Making the
Right Moves *in*
REAL
ESTATE

Making the
Right Moves *in*
REAL
ESTATE

An Insider's Guide
for Buyers and Sellers Seeking
the Best Answers to
Real Estate Questions

RICHARD ARDIA

FOREWORD BY BOB BECKER

Former Chairman and CEO of the National Real Estate Trust

MOONLIGHT PUBLISHING

Published by
Moonlight Publishing, LLC
2528 Lexington Street
Lafayette, CO 80026
www.moonlight-publishing.com

ISBN 0-9779603-2-3
ISBN 13: 978-0-9779603-2-3

Library of Congress Catalog Number applied for

Distributed by National Book Network

For my parents, Vincent and Anita Ardia,
I honor you now with deep appreciation for the support and
guidance you have always given me.

To my brother, Steve Ardia,
who has never wavered in his commitment
and dedication to being my brother and lifetime friend.

To my children, Allison, John, and Heather,
nothing has given me greater pride than calling you my children.
Thank you for your enthusiasm and unconditional
devotion to family.

To my grandchildren,
Cooper John Moore and Trevor Richard Moore,
you have brought so much joy to so many.

Special thanks to Steve Sullivan,
for passing the pen to my hand.

To Charles Peers, my publishing agent,
without your expertise, diligence, and dedication, this book would
never have become a reality.

CONTENTS

# FOREWORD

Serving as the Chairman and Chief Executive Officer of one of the largest real estate organizations in the world provided me an opportunity to experience thousands of real estate transactions totaling billions of dollars. I learned first hand how important the decisions are when it comes to buying and selling real estate. The sale and purchase of a home is a financial and highly charged emotional experience. Much has been written about the subject.

I have known Dick Ardia as both a good friend and a business associate. So, I must confess that when he told me he was writing a book on real estate, my first thought was, "How do you tell a friend the last thing the world needs is another book on how to make a fortune in real estate?" However, I should have known better. I should have known that anything Dick Ardia tackled would be original, thought provoking, humorous and most importantly, useful. You see, the author has this wonderful gift to be able to view things from different perspectives. He has the talent to demystify complex subjects and to present them in understandable and practical ways.

Real estate transactions can drain the most sophisticated buyers and sellers because there is so much at stake when we buy and sell our homes. For the first time, a book has been written to help the consumer navigate these potentially treacherous waters. Dick Ardia has lifted the veil to help you fully understand the process of selecting the right broker and "making all the right decisions" to insure a profitable and emotionally stable real estate transaction. He has kept his ear and his heart tuned into the needs of the consumer.

Drawing upon my own 40 years of experience, I can tell you that this book is a must read for every potential buyer and seller of real estate, regardless of whether it is your first or fifth experience. The fact is, most of us will be in both roles many times during our lifetimes. *Making the Right Moves in Real Estate* is chock full of good old fashion common sense and tempered with the realities of today's modern technologically advanced market place. It is a "How-to Roadmap" that will help you become a much more confident and competent buyer or seller. It is the consumers best guide ever to understanding the real estate world from the perspective of the buyer, seller, real estate agent and the techniques of marketing, that have been proven by historical performance.

When I read the book I felt like I was sitting in a room listening to Dick Ardia speak directly to me. He has the ability to provide so much information in a personal and conversational style. This book is an easy read because the author provides a unique blend of facts, anecdotes and humor, all of which will make the pages seem like they are turning themselves. I found myself smiling throughout the entire book. You will too. But the best and most important smile will be the one on your face at the conclusion of your next and most successful real estate transaction.

BOB BECKER
Former Chairman and Chief Executive Officer
NRT (National Real Estate Trust)

 # PREFACE

Book stores are filled with information on real estate. Some provide you with technical terms, definitions and basic fundamentals. Others are written without great practical experience. For the most part, they are accurate and helpful. The "how-to" group is geared to make you wealthy even if you have no knowledge, no experience, no job and no money. These books, along with television "infomercials," make it seem so easy that even your pets can own real estate. They certainly appear to qualify.

This book is not like any other. There is no get-rich-quick scheme. It will not teach you about different types of mortgages and other technical information. There is no glossary of terms and standard definitions. That kind of "textbook" information is readily available elsewhere. *Making the Right Moves in Real Estate* will clearly illustrate the proven principles and concepts of real estate. It will teach you the basic building blocks and how to apply them to real-life situations. It will show you the inner workings of buyers, sellers, and real estate agents. You will also learn about marketing, market conditions, and the financial aspects of buying and selling real estate. This book is intended to help everyone navigate their way through the real estate maze. It will also prove to be a worthy asset for real estate companies and their agents, regardless of their experience. It will build self-confidence and inspire you to believe in real estate, like never before.

Remember, just gathering information, without the commitment to apply it, is like practicing for a game that will never be played. Successful real estate ventures require knowledge, money and the determination to act swiftly. Knowledge is the easiest to acquire. Saving money requires discipline. Lack of commitment and the courage to act in a timely manner keeps many people from reaping all potential rewards.

We have all heard the "almost" battle cry. I should have. I could have. If I only knew then what I know now. Looking at these "near misses" in hindsight generally hurts. The view backwards, more times than not, serves to remind us that we should have followed our gut feelings. It provides a chance to reflect after the fact, when no elements of risk, reward or timing are at stake. The "stands are empty" and there is no scoreboard.

Successful transactions involve learning, preparation, and the courage to move forward. When these elements work together, they can provide the ingredients necessary to create what some people call "perfect timing." When this kind of timing occurs consistently, it involves none of the elements of chance. It is the result of a well planned event.

Everyone has to live somewhere. Lives can change by the minute. People get married. People get divorced. Retirement arrives and neighborhoods start to change. Families expand and contract. New lives are born each day and others are lost. We want large homes and then we want smaller homes. Incomes increase and decrease. Change is everywhere and it is the catalyst to real estate activity. Think about the life cycle of one person and how his or her real estate needs will evolve over a lifetime. Multiply that by millions of people and it is easy to see the enormous need for everyone to have a complete understanding of the concepts and inner workings of real estate. Real estate beckons the consumer to learn as much as possible because every transaction is critical in building lifetime assets.

Regardless of interest rates, market conditions, stock market gyrations and other economic and personal factors, the real estate "beat" goes on. Real estate is the largest single business in the world. Every company has to operate someplace and every person has to live somewhere. Call it residential, commercial, land sales, industrial or new construction, it does not matter because it all involves land, structures and people. This book "houses" the answers on how to accumulate and preserve wealth over a lifetime of real estate moves. Now let's turn the "key" and go inside.

THE FRONT DOOR INTRODUCTION:
FROM A TIN CAN TO A BOOK

In 1971 I received a holiday gift from a good friend. It was a nicely decorated tin can with a selection of gourmet popcorn inside. With kids and family around for the holidays, I am not sure I even tasted it, but apparently it was a big hit. When the treats were all gone, I went to throw the can away. However, having come from a long line of pack rats, I decided to keep it for some future use. You know the thinking, "Someday I will need a large container for something, heaven only knows what, but just in case, I will keep it anyway." After all, a trip to the attic was no big deal.

The very next year I changed careers and headed into the real estate business. Events started happening at a machine-gun like pace. My mind was filling with ideas, thoughts to remember and lessons I had never learned before. I guess if I was a computer, you could say my hard drive was getting full. I had a strong urge to save this information. Then one day I went to get something in the attic and saw that tin can. It sort of jumped over in front of me and said, "take me." So I did. I took it with me downstairs to my den and placed it next to my desk.

Then it "spoke" to me again. "Fill me up with every lesson and experience you have in business, family and life."

I smiled because now I had learned two things. First of all, it does pay to keep items around because you never know when you might need them. Secondly, here was a great method of storing away every important event that I was experiencing in my new career.

Beginning in 1972 I started writing down these notions on scraps of paper and tossing them into the popcorn tin. It included certain words people had said to me that made sense and that I wanted to remember. Actions of anyone around me that influenced my thinking got recorded and stored. Solutions to problems would end up in that little round can. Experiences learned from others were sure to make their way into the storage tank. Lessons learned the hard way went in on larger sheets of paper. Knowledge was coming at me quickly and that container started to fill up at a very fast pace. Over twenty-five years of direct real estate involvement with buyers, sellers, agents, attorneys and others helped provide a constant flow of material about people, situations, and outcomes.

I had no idea why I was doing this but somehow I thought all of these little pieces of paper would come in handy. Who knows, I might even write a book. What a crazy idea. Who would ever have the time to do that? Well, the next time I walked into a bookstore I knew the answer to that question. When I started writing this book 32 years later my best sources were the 182 notes stored in that holiday tin can. Interesting how things work out sometimes; going from "tin can alley" to this day has been quite a journey.

So here it is. A book about real estate, filled with big life lessons sprinkled throughout, like a great seasoning on your favorite dish.

During the process of writing this book I realized how much time must be devoted to making something like this happen. I gained enormous respect for every author that has ever written a book.

Over the past year this project has become a passion. It has taken over my everyday life. It has caused me to work twelve-hour days and sometimes all night too. I forgot what sleep was. At times I was exhausted from the efforts but I was never more energized and motivated. If my enthusiasm is contagious, then these pages will turn themselves and you will soon learn the importance of *Making the Right Moves in Real Estate.*

When It Rains It Pours....

It was raining hard that April night. I had just returned home from work and my family was packing for our annual spring vacation. The phone rang and the man on the line said his name was Sandy. I did not recognize the voice or name. He told me that I had written a note to his Dad about his father's house. Then it hit me. About eight months before I had been riding my bike past this wonderful old home. It was quite hidden from sight but with a little effort I could tell the "bones" were good. I saw an elderly gentleman working on a tree that had recently fallen. I asked him if he needed help. He promptly looked up and said, "no thanks," with a brisk turn of his head. I told him to have a good day and turned my bike around. He whistled and I looked back to see him give me a thumbs up. I signaled back the same and we both smiled. I went home and that night I wrote him a note telling him how much I loved his home and that if he ever wanted to sell it to please contact me.

Sandy informed me that his Dad had recently passed away. I felt badly even though I barely knew the man. He explained that his father had told him about the note I had written. He went on to say that he had instructed him to contact me if anything ever happened to him.

I knew Sandy's father for about one minute, but we obviously had made a connection. Sandy asked if I wanted to see the house. I had not even begun packing for our vacation and I was exhausted from work, but I left immediately in the pouring April rain. I inspected the home and got that "go for it" feeling in my gut. I bought the house that night at the kitchen table. The process took about two hours.

Sandy and I shook hands. That was good enough for both of us. I took the plot plans with me on vacation and designed a minor subdivision. Within ninety days from the closing of title, the town had approved the plan and I had a nice half-acre building lot. I held on to it for many years, following Will Rogers's advice to "buy land because they are not making any more of it."

The list of reasons for me not to have gone over to see that house was long and strong. On the other hand, if I had not gone I would have built a vantage point from which to exercise my own painful hindsight.

I rented the home and many years later sold the lot for more than I had paid for the entire property and the house. I continued to rent the home for many years. The value of the house is now four times what I paid for it, not including the money I got from the sale of the half-acre lot. The home that was built on the lot that I sold greatly improved the neighborhood and caused a positive acceleration of the price of my home. There is nothing like creating and controlling your own market.

That night I realized that just knowing basic real estate concepts is not enough. I was sure I knew all that had to be known. I had most of the technical answers. However, I did not realize that you have to be prepared to execute your plan when the opportunity presents itself. If it is inconvenient, make it convenient. If fear comes to the door, push it away with preparation, logic, and belief in yourself. Listening to others is fine up to a point. Too much opinion-seeking consumes valuable time. It is always best done prior to encountering the opportunity. Opportunities can be like trains; they stop at the station for a few minutes and wait for you to get on board. If you do nothing, the door closes and the train pulls away. That opportunity is going to someone else.

So why own real estate? After you have read this book, you will never ask yourself that question again.

Why Real Estate?

Shelter is a necessity, right up there with our need for food, air and water. We need to sleep somewhere each day. We need a home. Most of us start out by renting our first place. We may share this burden with others, but it is still rent. We quickly realize that renting allows us to burn a lot of cash with no chance of gain. There is usually a relationship between responsibility and reward. At certain times in our lives renting works as a transition step, but it is rarely the best long-term financial solution.

Many new buyers start off their home search by stating they do not want to be "house poor." They still want to continue to live and enjoy life. They do not want to put all their money into a home. Yes, it is true; being "house poor" is definitely not good, but if you don't own your own home you'll be experiencing a different kind of poverty.

Most of us know you have to sacrifice something to get ahead in life. Oftentimes we just need to be reminded of this principle and get a "little push" to get us going in the right direction.

There are few investments, if any, that can compare to real estate. Even if the financial returns of other types of investment instruments were identical or even better, I know of none that will allow you to live in it. In addition, just about everyone can become an expert because local knowledge is just that. When we live in our homes and participate in the community, we can become very knowledgeable about our town and its inner workings. All of this helps to provide a natural base for building your real estate knowledge.

Rarely is there a social gathering where the conversation does not include the activity of the local real estate market. Real estate interests everyone, and owning what you know the most about—your home—is good business. Real estate is tangible and understandable.

One day my youngest daughter Heather asked me why I spend so much time working at my desk. She was only ten years old, but she had a lot of natural curiosity. I knew she wanted a real answer, so I told her I was working on my real estate properties. Then she asked me why I like real estate so much. I told her that I loved different styles of homes and I loved land.

That is why I own several properties, not just the one we live in now. She smiled and gave me a hug and asked me if she could have a property, too. I put my pen down and left the room because I knew it was not going to get any better than that.

1 THE BASIC PRINCIPLES OF REAL ESTATE

An "I.R.A." That's Worth Its Weight in "Sold"

Millions of homeowners have built their "nest eggs" by owning real estate. They probably did not realize it would turn out that way, but it did. Over the long run, homes continue to build value while we enjoy living in them. Real estate has turned out to be another form of an individual retirement account (I.R.A.). It is a fact that when millions of Americans get ready to retire, the value of their real estate assets makes a significant difference in their ability to live comfortable lives. Moving to an area where they can get more for their money actually allows some people to increase their home amenities and put cash in the bank.

The monthly discipline of paying down a mortgage and building equity pays off. Combined with the annual tax savings advantages, home owners can build quite a home savings account. Something worth its weight in "sold," when the time is right. At the heart of most family estates are the real estate assets.

Tax Laws Favor and Flavor Real Estate Ownership

Current tax laws provide many benefits for home owners. Please seek advice from your accountant for specific benefits and updates as to how they apply to your individual tax returns. However, the following general principles are valid as of this writing;

- The interest paid on a mortgage is deductible every year. Up to $1,000,000 in mortgage debt on a first and second home is fully deductible.
- Interest up to $100,000 is deductible on home equity loans.
- Annual real estate taxes paid on first and second home properties are deductible items.
- Capital improvements. When you make major improvements to your home you gain at least three ways. First of all, improvements to your kitchens, baths, family rooms and other areas more than likely will bring increased desirability to your home. That translates into more market value for you and perhaps a quick sale when the time comes to sell. Second, you will be able to use the costs of capital improvements to increase your initial cost basis when you sell. (Maintenance and normal repairs are not added to your cost basis.) Third, you get to enjoy your improvements.

Current tax laws favor home ownership. As of this writing the tax law allows a single person to make up to $250,000 in profit without paying any taxes. Married couples can make up to $500,000 in profit. There are certain conditions that have to be met but basically you have to be dealing with your prime residence and the seller has to have occupied it for a total of at least two of the last five years prior to the closing date. The current tax law allows you to continue to do this over and over again, provided you do not use the exemption more than once every two years.

Refinancing and Home Equity Provide Cash Flow

When you build equity in your home it allows you to borrow money. Equity is the value of your home, minus any debts you owe on the house. All you have to do is pick up any newspaper in your town to see that banks cannot wait to lend you cash for your home improvements. This alone is an enormous vote of confidence for real estate. Conservative financial institutions love real estate.

Most banks do not figure the net value of your home after a sale when doing an appraisal for loan purposes. If you sold a property and paid a commission, your net equity would be the sales price less the commission, other related closing costs, and the amount of the loan balances due at closing. Most lenders do not include the cost of a commission or the cost of necessary repairs in their appraisals for home equity loans. That allows you to have even more borrowing power. Let's assume a bank will lend money for a first mortgage and a home equity line covering up to 80% of the value of the home. If they appraise the house for $600,000 that means they would allow qualified lenders a total debt service of $480,000. If the bank subtracted an agent's fee of 5% off the "market value," that would allow 80% of $570,000 or $456,000. Therefore the $480,000 figure provides an additional $24,000 in borrowing power. That can be enough for a year's college tuition or a new car.

Your Own Savings and Loan Is Always Open

When you borrow money on your house you do not have to pay any taxes on the money you receive. (Some limitations may apply). This is a financial tax advantage that gives most homeowners 100% use of their money. The key is that you are borrowing from your own asset and no "sale" has taken place. If you sell stocks, bonds, or any other investment instrument and make a profit, you will more than likely have to pay capital gains taxes, unless you have losses to offset these gains. Paying taxes on profits reduces your actual working capital. As your home increases in value, you have started to build your own savings and loan department. If you need money, your equity growth may help to pay tuition, medical bills, or provide the money necessary for home improvements.

The extended length of term for the payback allows the monthly payment to remain low compared to other short term loans. Many home owners use home equity loans to consolidate and reduce other debts while actually lowering their monthly payments. Many a college student went off to school fueled by the cash from a home equity loan. The interest paid is deductible, which can make the actual loan rate even lower and you get the full amount of the money borrowed. Not as good as a scholarship, but a very attractive means of borrowing for college educations and keeping the monthly payments reasonable.

2 LEVERAGE CAN HELP BUILD WEALTH

When you make a down payment on real estate, combined with a mortgage loan, you are able to purchase an item worth many times your actual cash layout. Think about it. If you buy a home for $400,000 and you put 20% down, your cash outlay is $80,000. So your 20% has allowed you to leverage your money into a purchase that is worth five times your cash investment. Now it gets even better. If a home appreciates 6% each year, you get 6% of $400,000 figure, not just your $80,000 down payment. That difference is significant. Six percent of $80,000 is $4,800. Six percent of $400,000 is $24,000. You are gaining $19,200 more because you leveraged your money. As the years go on, the gain in this difference continues to get wider. For example, in year two, you would get 6% of $424,000 or $25,440 as compared to 6% of $84,800, which is $5,088. The difference is $20,352. Remember the interest earned on your cash would have been taxable, therefore reducing the actual return. Equity growth remains safe from taxes until the time of sale and with single and married deductions allowing profits of $250,000 and $500,000 respectively, for most sellers there are no taxes payable. Now you can see why owning real estate is a wealth builder and the cornerstone of most individual estates.

The Value of a Mortgage Is Often Understated

Without a mortgage most people wouldn't be able to buy a home. Yes, you can pay a lot of interest over a long period of time, but if you did not buy a home, you could pay a lot of rent over a long period as well and build no equity.

There is simply no comparison between twenty years of home ownership and twenty years of renting. Shelter is not optional for most people. It is a necessity. If you decide not to buy, you have also made the decision to rent or live with family. Neither has proven to be a good long-term solution. Look at a mortgage as the best financial instrument available. A mortgage is the reason you can leverage your money. It is a loan against what you own. You hold the house deed and the bank has a lien against your property. It is a legally recorded loan and upon a sale of the premises, it must be paid off. Compare this to an auto loan where you borrow the money and the bank owns the car. They keep the title to the car until you pay off the loan. You own nothing but a big debt and an item that depreciates as soon as you say "give me the keys."

I think it is fair to say that lending institutions feel secure in providing home mortgages. (Try getting a loan for a new restaurant or a bike shop!) Most loan qualifying ratios applied today are based on the ability of the borrower to pay back the debt. With even modest gains in home values along with monthly reduction of principal, the risk to the bank lessens as time moves on. However, during markets that turn downward, the bank has the greatest risk of all.

Lending Institutions Are the Backbone

Who else would lend you 80, 85, 90, and even 95% of the value of something? You can buy a home with 5% down and even nothing down in some cases. But here is the best part. With a standard mortgage, when you sell the home for three times what you paid for it, the bank only wants back the balance due on the original loan amount. You keep all the profits. Think about that business deal.

Can you imagine going into a joint venture with someone whereby you lend them 80% of the money, you take most of the risk, and five years later when the business venture or real estate sells for $150,000 more than what it cost, all you get back is the balance on the money you loaned out? Your partner keeps all the profits. It is easy to see why lending institutions are the backbone of real estate in the U.S.

In addition, for all the years of the loan, the borrowers are able to deduct the interest paid on their tax return and the lender must treat the interest paid to them as income. Tax deductible interest can result in reducing the actual loan interest rate cost by 20, 30, or even 40%, depending on the borrower's tax bracket. A 6% loan rate can easily become a 4 % loan rate to the borrower. Lending institutions are responsible for helping millions of home owners build wealth.

Supply and Demand Determine Value

What would you pay for a glass of water if you had been in the desert for ten days? Cruel as this may sound, it demonstrates supply and demand in simple terms. It is not the number of items available that matters; it is the number of people ("demand") who desire those items that drives value. If you had thousands of gallons of water in the desert but no one needed water, what do you think the price of water would be? An item for which there is no demand will not sell. Real estate is all about supply and demand. The same house in one state can sell for thousands of dollars more in another because of supply and demand.

Our population is growing. People are living longer, and better. As the average life span increases, people remain in their homes for longer periods of time. This actually keeps properties from coming back on the market. It causes a shortage of homes. People get used to a place and do not want to give it up. Families have changed over the last few decades. Children grow up, go to college and, in many cases, return home to live with parents for several years. The need for keeping the family home can continue for many years past what was originally planned.

At the same time so-called "baby boomers" continue to drive the need for housing. Combined incomes of the modern couple have increased buying power significantly over the years. In addition, second home ownership is growing quickly in many parts of the country. Find an ocean, mountain, lake, club, ski resort, or golf course and you will find a cluster of second homes. One home is not enough for a growing number of people.

They Are Not Making Any More of It

As Will Rogers stated, "they" may not be making any more land, but "they" are reclaiming lots that are currently occupied by outdated homes.

When the supply of land diminishes, builders tend to buy smaller and older homes that sit on large lots. What they see is a great building lot with an "obstruction" on it. They take the house down and build a new one. When this happens, it is positive proof that demand for land has outrun the supply. In some of these hot market areas, where older homes sit on a great site, the land actually represents almost the entire value of the real estate. The local town government may still separate the assessed value by improvements and land, but in these high demand land markets, it is the land that has taken over almost the entire value. When builders buy a property and immediately knock down the structure sitting on it, they are providing positive proof that the true value is in the land. Many land locations once considered useless have been recovered, and with sound planning and protective laws in place, have become sites for major developments.

3 LOCATION CREATES THE BEST VALUE

One of the most familiar statements concerning real estate has always been "location, location, location." It is the classic answer to the question, "When you buy real estate, what are the three most important things to consider?" It has long been realized that core value of all real estate begins with location.

Every piece of land is valued by its specific location and its relationship to its immediate surroundings. A nice half-acre parcel in one town can sell for $200,000 where 25 miles away an even nicer three-acre parcel can sell for $100,000. Why? Let's begin with the "center of influence" theory. Just about everything is affected by its immediate surroundings. The closer you are to a positive center of influence, the better the location, and vice-versa. Thus, the better your location is compared to others, the more desirable your property becomes.

The quality of the town or city development, employment opportunities, master plans, closeness to basic amenities, quality of life issues, schools, transportation, safety concerns, environmental issues, shopping and consumer conveniences, local zoning ordinances, closeness to water, views and supporting values, all can add or subtract to the value of a particular location.

In real estate, value is relative. Properties sell for less or more because of location, condition, style, center of influences, curb appeal, supporting values, and supply and demand. However, not all homes and locations appeal to the same to all people. That is one reason that there are few vacant homes. In most cases, a great home in a poor location has less appeal than a mediocre home in a great location. When you have a high quality home on an exceptional property and it is set in a highly desirable town, you are in the best position to sell at the top market price. During hot seller markets, even multiple offers will come in and create an auction-like atmosphere for high demand homes.

You can change a lot of things in a home, but location is not one of them. However, if and when key elements of value and positive center of influences come together, what were once considered to be poor locations can be transformed quickly. Urban renewal can create huge opportunities for growth. Then again, sometimes just the revitalization of a street can be a positive influence on surrounding home values.

Home Ownership Builds Pride

Most of us like to work hard and own certain assets that help make life more enjoyable for our friends and family. Our home and our cars represent two such assets. When you have something to show for your efforts you feel good. You feel proud. You enjoy the benefits of hard work and sacrifice. Many of us also like others to see what we have. Pride can surface in many ways. It can show up as new furniture, a new lawnmower, a new kitchen or a new house. Pride of ownership can also be felt in many small ways. It can be sitting in front of your fireplace on a Sunday morning, mowing your lawn, entertaining friends and family at a barbeque, planting flowers, or simply relaxing in the comfort and beauty of your own surroundings. Feeling proud is a good feeling. Homes have a natural way of expressing their charm and providing a sense of security.

Nothing compares to nature's beauty, but home ownership compliments it well. Owning is different than renting; it's difficult to take full pride in something you don't own, and for which you must rely on a stranger to maintain.

How Interest Rate Changes Affect the Real Estate Market

During the 1980s the country had some of the highest interest rates in its history. A prime rate of 21% and mortgage rates that topped 18% were killing the market for buyers and sellers alike. During that time prices of homes kept coming down. Supply outran demand because fear of high mortgage payments kept many buyers out of the market. The stock market crash in 1987 changed the financial landscape for many. Even if you were not directly affected, it was a "shot heard around the world." Every time the rate went up, thousands of buyers were taken out of the market place. We heard this over and over from the news media. The market swelled with homes and it became a true buyers market, often defined as a time when there are an abundance of homes on the market and the sellers have little negotiating leverage, doing whatever it takes to make a sale happen. Every market place has its own "tides" and timetable.

Generally speaking, when rates head downward more buyers qualify to purchase and enter the market place. At first, that causes an increase in the number of homes leaving the market. If rates continue to drop, buyer demand increases and eventually supply shortages press prices upward. Lower interest rates have always been one of the main "teases" to get buyer attention.

A Buyer's Market May Not Always Be What It Appears

Real estate values and demand vary greatly throughout the country. Sometimes when there are lots of homes to choose from, it appears to be a buyer's market. However, this is not always true because if there is no long-term demand in an area, homes keep coming on the market and prices keep falling. This has happened in certain cities and rural areas. Sometimes it is simply physical deterioration of an area or the removal of a center of influence that can make this happen. Remember, not all areas of the market respond the same to current economic conditions. Real estate is as local as local can get and because of that, you must be aware of the current conditions in the area you are seeking to live in.

When a major employer either moves into or leaves an area, it can have a profound impact on the surrounding community. Keep in mind that history has shown that eventually, after many years of a downward trend in values, a reversal can occur. Then the "gold rush mentality" may run wild because what was once thought of as useless real estate now begins to look good again. It may take decades for this to happen, but land that is within the reach of major centers of influence will prove to hold significant value again and again.

A Seller's Market Can Be Confusing for Buyers

In a seller's market interest rates are usually low and real estate prices high. Houses sell quickly, keeping the supply of homes on the lean side. Buyers become anxious and find themselves losing out on homes they take too long to bid on. The irony is that buyers are paying more for a home at a time when interest rates may be at their lowest. This all seems to point to the conclusion that people will pay whatever the market demands in price as long as they get a low interest mortgage.

However, those who buck this trend most likely will end up with a property that appreciates in value at a greater rate, and perhaps a lower mortgage rate as a result of refinancing.

During the high interest rate periods of twenty-five years ago most people were filled with apprehension. Everything that they knew about real estate went out the window because of higher mortgage rates. After all, who would want a mortgage with rates in the teens? Many successful investors know that in many cases the time to buy is when others think it is not the right time. Going against the grain takes a bit more work but the rewards can be outstanding. Real estate maintains a good balance for those who want to find it and have the courage to act while others retreat from the market.

Going Against the Grain Takes More Effort

Buying during a period of high interest rates can be even more lucrative to the buyer if the mortgage market is on the verge of reversing its position. As the buyers' market strengthens, purchasers may be able to buy homes for ten to thirty percent less than when interest rates were at lower levels.

They pay less for the homes and because of that, end up with a smaller mortgage. Yes, the mortgage may be at a high rate, but in a few years the opportunity to re-finance will soften that rate and the original purchase price will look even better.

For example, a buyer who was able to purchase a home for $300,000 might have paid $340,000 for the same home a few years earlier when the rates were lower and the seller's market was at a peak. In a buyer's market the interest rate tends to be much higher on the mortgage, but the actual amount of that mortgage will be less.

Assuming the down payment remains the same, the mortgage amount in this example would be $40,000 less. If the buyer had paid $340,000 for the home when rates were at 7%, the monthly mortgage payments for $240,000 on a 30-year loan would have been $1,596 per month. With the increase in rates and a change to a buyer's market, the purchase of the same home at $300,000 would yield a mortgage of $200,000 at 10% for 30 years. The monthly payment for this loan would be $1,754, leaving a difference of only $158 more per month.

In a few years rates could come down, providing an opportunity to refinance. While it would cost approximately $4,000 dollars more in payments (part of which is principal payback) over two years, the house's value could rise by as much as 10%, which would give the home owner $30,000 more in equity—a net gain of approximately $26,000. Not bad. In some cases the cost of refinancing is insignificant compared to the gain in equity. Guidelines for refinancing are available at any mortgage lender. Generally speaking, if you do not plan to stay in your house very long, or the rate decrease is not enough to justify the cost, then holding on to your existing rate may make some sense for the short term. In either case, if rates are going down, values will start to increase as more buyers enter the marketplace. Appreciation will begin to accelerate. Even with a 3% annual appreciation on a $300,000 home, the annual increase in value is $9,000.

Changing markets have provided many astute buyers the opportunity to refinance their homes, gain acceleration in home values and only carry that high-rate "30-year" loan for a few years, not 30 years. Mortgage interest is tax deductible, and in each case the actual cost of the loan is decreased by this tax advantage. Buyers bold enough to act during periods of high interest rates have a large inventory to choose from. During strong seller markets, buyers have fewer homes to select from and may even have to settle for less than they really wanted. Also keep in mind that during seller markets, you have to be fast as Jesse James to get your offer in ahead of the others. Going against the grain may be a pain but it also might provide a fabulous gain!

The Relationship Between Rental Income and Market Conditions

If you are renting it is important to keep in mind that the rental market also has changing "tides." This is true for both tenants paying rent and the landlords who own the properties. Supply and demand is active in the rental markets as well. With every change in market conditions some segments of real estate gain ground while others lose. A see-saw effect can occur and because of that, real estate investments can provide a very balanced growth advantage.

During strong seller's markets, rental incomes on

residential investment properties may suffer. As interest rates continue to fall, more and more buyers enter the marketplace. Fewer people have to rent. When this happens more rental properties come on and stay on the market, causing an oversupply. If the seller's market continues for a sustained period of time, rents may stagnate or start to come down because of low demand.

On the other hand, the value of the actual properties will be increasing due to strong demand. If you own an investment property, selling during this time period might be a good move. After all, you are both a landlord and a seller. You can gain maximum rental income during periods of rental shortages and then sell the property when the values are highest. In most cases the investment ownership of real estate is diversified in its ability to adjust to the peaks and valleys of economic conditions. Tax advantages for real estate investors are substantial, and while rental income pays down mortgage balances, the landlord also reaps the benefits of principal reduction, depreciation (which is tax deductible) and the appreciation of the dwelling's value.

Real Estate Is a Segmented Market

Residential real estate is a highly segmented market: not all price ranges are affected the same during the same economic conditions.

Residential real estate, like the stock market, requires more than one answer to the question, "How is the market doing?"

As national economic conditions change not all regions are affected the same by inflation, appreciation, employment, and other factors. National figures can be misleading when applied to regional, state, and local communities. It would be a mistake to use any of that information without understanding the local conditions.

Real Estate Is as Local as Local Gets

The best rule of thumb to follow is to know your local market. Find out what is happening in all price ranges. Seek only closed file information, not opinions. Opinions are very often "old news," depending on the source, and often biased.

Become educated about the conditions that apply directly to the area you are buying or selling properties. Inactivity does not necessarily occur across the board. Ask specific questions. How is the upper end of the market doing? What is the hottest price range right now? How many days is it taking for the average home to sell? All of these questions will give you a feel for the marketplace and the price range you are seeking. Average number of days on the market tells more about the home market than all the expert opinions condensed into one. Facts are facts and opinions are opinions. Although opinions cost nothing, following the wrong ones can be very costly.

Commercial, industrial, and land sales require similar questions to determine how each segment of the market is reacting.

4 NEEDS, WANTS, AND DESIRES
CREATE BUYERS

Up to this point, you have read about the basic principles of residential real estate, as these concepts apply to the majority of buyers and sellers. Knowing and understanding these principles is a must for everyone. Each day certain life events take place causing real estate to move. People make changes in their lives and sometimes changes are made for them. We all know the rule of the "three-pack;" good events and bad events seem to occur in groups of threes and when they do, something is going to change. The outcome of certain "people events" may cause real estate to change hands.

People move real estate and real estate moves people. When a home is too large or too small, or lacking certain amenities, the home causes people to seek new space.

Homes have the power to inspire market movement. Every time you visit a friend's house that you love, you are seeing and experiencing the "magnetic pull" of real estate. Unlike most other products, though, homes are everywhere. Real estate can make people move. It can make you want to add on an addition or move to a new home. When you visit your friends and see their new family room with the fireplace burning, those gentle warm flames can whisper to you, "this is for me."

Watching a new home go up in the neighborhood creates a lot of interest, too. Many people find themselves walking around the construction site and dreaming a little for themselves. There are a variety of reasons people desire to increase their home amenities. Certain physical needs may require a move, but wanting to be proud of your home is one of the strongest motivators of all.

Forget the Excuses

For many activities in life it pays to practice and be prepared for opportunities before they knock at your door. Generally speaking, when we are not prepared to take action, we tend to make excuses in order to rationalize our lack of commitment to act.

Excuses like these can cancel knowledge and preparation: "If I only had the time to think this over, I could make a decision." "If I could check with my banker, then I would make a move." "If I could call my Dad I would feel better." "If I was only sure of my raise, I would not hesitate." When the "if" word starts off your sentences, you may be allowing apprehension to dominate your logic. Buying real estate is a highly emotional experience for most people. It can be like falling in love. At the moment you realize you have found the house of your dreams, your knees get a little weak and logic starts to leaves you as the "heartbeats of anticipation" increase.

Knowledge, preparation, and determination can all be replaced with excuses. As excuses start to appear, the more likely it is that fear is taking over. Think of those "excuses" as being weights. Imagine if every time you made an excuse, a five-pound weight was hung around your neck. After a while you would be lucky if you could even walk. And with your head pulled down, how could you possibly see any opportunities right in front of you? Excuses kill "vision."

Forget the excuses. The checklist of legal help, vendors, and inspectors lined up to protect you after you make a decision is growing every year. Courage can only be measured against the opportunity and the risk at hand. Remember, our fears can be like bandits that snatch our confidence and undermine our actions.

Preparation and a clear personal business plan can help eliminate fear. You must know what you are doing before you find yourself in the emotional turmoil of making a decision. The Boy Scouts had it figured out a long time ago. Be Prepared.

Without Preparation, Life Can Be Like a Ride in the Clothes Dryer

Most people do not like to sit down and write out a personal business plan. On the other hand, most of us would not want to work for a company that did not have one. However, when it comes to buying or selling properties I cannot overemphasize the importance of this step. Your personal balance sheet will open your eyes to your strengths and weaknesses. Recognize each for what it is, and in most cases build an action plan to correct any weak areas. Soft spots such as debt service, bad credit, no credit, job security, poor saving patterns, small down payments, and personal issues that will block opportunities are not going to help you buy a home. Making positive adjustments in advance is a key part of buyer preparation.

Self-improvement only happens when we accept our

weaknesses and want to correct them. If you knew a tennis player that had a great forehand but a very weak backhand, what advice would you have for her? Obviously, the most meaningful words would be to tell her to improve her weakest area, her backhand stroke. Compliments directed at her strengths would not help. This is a good example of how we improve ourselves in life, by strengthening our weakest areas. Eliminate the excuses and defensive mechanisms that can block meaningful learning opportunities and pave the way for self-improvement. This line of thinking can work for anyone desiring to enhance his or her financial balance sheet as well other areas of his or her life.

If you have been a poor saver for years, you can break that bad habit. Recognize this as a weakness and build a mini-business plan to correct it. Many buyers, when properly focused by a quality agent or family member, have saved a great deal of money in a relatively short period of time. If you really want a home, the sacrifice is worth it. Discipline is the word that can make it work. Having that check book loaded and ready to fire is the only way to enter the market place. Disciplined savings is the best way to prove you are serious about your home search. If the anchor does not hold, the boat will continue to drift in any direction.

Buying with a Spouse or Partner? Share Knowledge

If there is more than one person involved in the buying process, try to do as much as you can together. Do not leave the other person out of the learning curve. Many times when transferees are involved in the buying process, the party being transferred views all the homes. They communicate on the phone what they have seen and what they have learned. Pictures can be exchanged and visual tours taken but that may or may not be sufficient when it comes to liking a home and learning about a new area. Oftentimes after finding a great house the transferee arranges for the other party to view the house.

The best relocation agents know they must first educate all buyers about market values, schools, amenities, and town advantages before they look at any homes. They have to bring both people up to the same speed. This can soften the blow of hitting that new market head-on with little explanation. Real estate is tangible, and all the pictures and talk will not compare to one on-site visit of a town and specific properties. Sometimes the learning process has to start all over again when both buyers are present. Even local buyers should look and learn together.

Get Pre-Approved by a Professional

Gather as much information as you can about your personal assets and liabilities. Most people spend a lot of time preparing their annual income tax returns. The effort and time expended are critical in order to gain the greatest refund or lessen the chances of owing more money. Before you decide to purchase or sell real estate, maintain this same kind of focus in developing a clear and accurate statement showing all of your assets and liabilities.

Contact a mortgage broker before you have selected an agent to look at homes. Even if real estate agents know how to qualify you, they are not arranging the loans and their primary focus is finding you a home. Go to the mortgage source first. It is neutral ground and will help clearly identify your financial potential. Many real estate brokers have this service available within their offices. Use it. It is important that you take your personal balance sheet to a mortgage lender and become pre-qualified to buy a home. Do not hide any information. The purpose is not to look as good as you can; it is to be truthful and find out what you have to do to obtain the mortgage amount you need. Correcting your weakest areas can turn out to be your greatest strength.

Mortgage professionals will show you how much you can afford. By adding the amount of mortgage funds available to your down payment, you can establish the price range for your home search. You will also need to have ample cash for the closing costs. Seek the information about closing costs at the time you are getting qualified. They can vary by each state and therefore there is no one answer for all. Always ask up front what the legal costs are going to be and all other purchase or seller costs directly related to a specific transaction. An important part of planning involves avoiding surprises.

Keep in mind that there are other costs that can vary. For example, taxes on the same priced homes can differ from town to town. So do the services. Paying more real estate taxes does not mean you are getting bad value. In some towns there are city sewers for which you may pay a special charge. However, if you find a home with a septic system, you just might have a large repair bill coming your way. Real estate property taxes, like most other things, represent certain values. Seek this information. Do not just ask what the taxes are. Ask, what do I get for my taxes? Taxes pay for items such as school systems, parks, police, and fire protection. Because taxes are paid annually, higher real estate taxes can affect your monthly payment substantially. A $3,000 annual difference in taxes on similarly priced homes can mean a monthly increase in your payment of $250. Real estate carrying costs are not the same for homes purchased at the same price. Property taxes, maintenance fees, insurance costs, and other costs may vary from state to state, town to town, and homeowners association to homeowners association. Ask your realtor for the information in your particular search area.

Seek Gifts from Family Prior to Looking for a Home

If you intend to ask family members for any additional funds to enhance your down payment, do so in advance of finding the right home. This is very important and the only fair way for all parties. First of all, you are buying the home, not your parents or friends. If you wait until you find that special home to ask for financial help, you place an additional burden on the people that might lend you the money. They may now feel they have to approve the entire purchase process.

In many instances first-time buyers fall in love with a house and then ask parents to come see the property, hoping they will like it as well and then lend them the money. This is fraught with problems. If your parents have not been in tune with current real estate values in your price range, they may react poorly to the home you are showing them. In that case there may be additional pressure for you to pass on a house you liked so much. It is hard for anyone to go from the armchair to appraiser of real estate values in one move.

To keep this from happening, get a commitment from your personal lender before you fall in love with a place not knowing whether or not you can afford it. This works best for all parties and is actually a relief for the family. This will clear the way for you to make a decision on a home without having to give the entire family the "tour." Save that program for after you have made your decision. Follow your gut feelings. It is your decision and all the consumer protections are there to help you make sure you made the right choices.

In most situations the mortgage lender will want to get a gift letter from any person giving you the money. The bank wants to be sure it is a gift and not a loan that requires payments of principal and interest.

Sellers Want That Pre-Approval Letter

In many of today's markets, sellers will not accept an offer from a buyer that has not been pre-qualified or pre-approved. Going house-hunting without a business plan is not a good idea. As you continue to save money for your down payment or if your basic income or debt service changes, be sure to get your qualification letter updated.

Establish credit and be sure it is in good standing. Car payments can hurt your borrowing power significantly. Many people do not think about that when they lease or buy a car with high monthly payments. Car payments are usually based on a three or four year payout. The short term makes the monthly payments high. That is why when you get ready to purchase a home that car payment can limit the amount you can borrow on your mortgage. Knowing exactly what the bank plans to lend you prepares you to act when that "opportunity train" stops at your station. One of the sharpest tools in the buyer's tool box is the pre-qualified loan approval letter. Don't look for a home without it.

Delaying Your Decision to Enter the Market
Can Cost You Money and Convenience

Let's use the simple example of Mary and Bill, first time home buyers. They have $50,000 to place down on a home. The price range they are looking for is $325,000-$350,000. They more than qualify for a $300,000 mortgage. Let's assume that homes continued to appreciate at 8% a year in many areas of the country. That means that in one year a $325,000 house would be selling for close to $350,000, an increase in value of about $25,000 in one year. If the buyers were able to save another $10,000 during that year they would have $60,000 to put down. Now if they waited a year and purchased that home for $350,000, they would end up with a $290,000 mortgage. If they did not save anything the situation would have been even more unfavorable.

The year before they could have bought a home for $325,000 with $50,000 down and a mortgage of only $275,000. In addition, the tax saving on deductible real estate taxes and mortgage interest might have meant paying less overall income tax for the year. Time is money and money is time—wasting either is not in your best interests.

When you buy real estate you can build equity, and you can build tax savings from your home deductions on interest and property taxes. The longer you own your home the further south your debt service travels. At the same time, even with modest appreciation, your market value heads north. The greater the distance between these two factors, the more equity you have earned. Equity is built by the increase in market value, key property improvements and the payoff of principal on the mortgage. This assumes the debt service remains the same.

Over the short run and the long run, waiting to buy real estate is usually not a wise choice. Rent has no investment potential for the tenant, only the landlord. If all elements of the market stayed the same and a potential buyer paid $20,000 in rent during a year they could have purchased a home, the reality of "burning dollars" becomes self evident.

Information on Home Sales May Not Be Accurate

For most of us real estate is a local game. We all live somewhere and consequently there is an abundance of real estate information available. However, not all of it is factual. People love to talk about homes on the market. Real estate is a hot topic at many social gatherings. However, much of the local information passed around may or may not be totally reliable. Remember, in real estate being off by 5% could be $25,000 or more. Like the old telephone game, when one person re-tells a story, the original message can get hopelessly altered.

Do not make decisions based on real estate data gathered from neighbors. For example. they may tell you they "got close to our asking price," which can mean 5-10% less than the original asking price. Remember, when a home comes on the market everyone thinks of its listed price as *the* price to compare their home's value to. Months later the price may have come down, but few people other than realtors realize this. So when neighbors or friends tell you that they got "close to our price," you don't know if they mean close to the original price or close to the reduced price. Only the closed files tell the truth. They are public information and recent sales are often posted in local papers. A realtor would also have this information, of course.

When you start your search for a home or your pursuit of a sale, try to keep an open mind as to current conditions. Conditions may have changed recently and like golf, real estate makes you play your ball where it lies, not where you want it to be.

Agents Can Vary Like the Adirondack Weather

As in most other fields, real estate agents vary in skills. There are good ones, bad ones, great ones, and those in a career transition. The best companies spend significant amounts of money and time on agent training and customer service issues. They also want managers who do not list and sell homes. It is very hard to help others when you are competing with them. Full-time managers should be there to support the agents and the clients. The best ones act as coaches, and even top salespeople can benefit from their broad perspective. Management support can provide tremendous advantages for home buyers, agents, and sellers. If your agent is not available, you have the manager to back up the transaction. Simple math tells us that two has more value than one.

For the most part, real estate agents are independent contractors and therefore work for themselves. For many years the field was filled with part-time agents who used real estate to supplement income and provide them with flexible working hours. This started to change in the 1970s, much to the benefit of the consumer. Throughout the next few decades the drive for full-time, trained agents dominated the real estate business in large metropolitan areas. Today, most successful companies will not hire anyone interested in part-time agent work.

Keep in mind that being full-time at anything does not in any way imply that the person is knowledgeable, dependable, and worthy of your business. However, regardless of knowledge, part-time involvement is simply not enough effort to keep pace with the real estate business.

Most Real Estate Transactions Are Big Deals

Real estate is big business, and every transaction is large compared to most of our other lifetime purchases. Requirements to become licensed are not that difficult, but honesty, integrity, determination, a strong work ethic, and loyalty are not qualities that can be tested for on a real estate exam.

Finding the best possible agent is the most critical step you will ever take. If you simply start with someone who you know socially you may be in for a bad real estate experience and the loss of a friendship. Your real estate "moves" require that you make business performance the number one objective. You can have a fully knowledgeable agent who communicates openly and honestly and who can obtain great results if you do not fall into the old patterns of selecting a broker through social contact. This is not to say that a personal contact may not be your best choice, but don't make that move without testing the other opportunities as well.

Don't Play "Real Estate Roulette"

Every day thousands of buyers call on ads in the newspaper or walk into real estate offices seeking information on a particular home. Many of the ads make a house sound, quite literally, too good to be true. That's what piques a buyer's interest and makes him want to seek answers.

Subconsciously buyers respond to ads because they think they've stumbled across a bargain. Brokers advertise to make the phone ring. Their job is to attract clients. But seldom do they ever sell the home that the buyer originally called about. They may show the house, but after talking with the customer, they will probably take him to another house that better fits his needs. When you call or stop into a real estate office the process usually starts by speaking with whoever is on "up time" in the office. Pick a number and you have an agent. This may work at the local bakery, but it can also be "Real Estate Roulette." This happens every day throughout the country, and people wonder why finding a home or selling a home can often become a rough ride. Remember, the goal of the sales agent is to get the buyer or seller into the office. Your goal is to find the best agent. Make sure you are riding your horse, not theirs. You should enter an office looking to conduct a search for the best agent, not signing up with whoever happens to be there at the time.

Can you imagine starting a search for an item that could involve hundreds of thousands of dollars with someone you know nothing about? Talk about rolling the dice! It would be like calling a hospital after an accident and asking whoever answered the phone to perform surgery. The single biggest investment most people will ever make should not begin with a spin of the wheel. Hours of personal time can be wasted, and many buyers can end up losing valuable market time because they did not make broker selection the most important step. Real estate roulette is not a game you want to play. The stakes are too high and the odds are not in your favor.

BROKER SELECTION IS THE "KEY" TO OPENING ALL THE RIGHT DOORS

5

If you owned a company and needed a graphic designer you might place an ad in a variety of media outlets. You could post it on the internet. You could place it in the local newspaper or a specific trade journal. After gathering a list of candidates, you would conduct an interview and select the two or three best candidates. Most employers would then proceed with an even more intense interview to determine who would get the job. This makes good business sense. It is done everyday all across the country. Why not follow the same kind of path when you are ready to buy or sell real estate? Too much work? Would you rather work with a friend, or the first person you met at a real estate office? I don't think so. After all, if you are going to use an agent, you want to select from the best companies with the best agents to obtain the best results.

To begin with, think of yourself as the "employer" when you are ready to select an agent. The more time and effort you put into the agent selection process, the better the chances for success in your buying and selling ventures. Keep in mind that if you do not know where you are going then you will not be working in your own best interests.

Unfortunately, more times than not, the selection of

an agent is made only because of personal familiarity with someone in the business. Everyone knows someone in the real estate business. Most of us know more than one agent and that alone should be a warning sign of the importance of doing a quality search. Real estate agents are ubiquitous. Sometimes a selection is made because the agent is attractive or just easy to be with. Sometimes it is for of social reasons. I do not think these qualifications alone would be enough to select a doctor for open heart surgery. Nor should they be the only criteria for agent selection.

Always be sure to select an agent that has the designation of "realtor" or "realtor- associate". That designation can only be used by an active member of the National Association of Realtors (NAR). All members must adhere to a strict Code of Ethics and Standards of Practice. This national organization has worked consistently to raise standards of practice and self-monitors any violations of their benchmark levels of professionalism.

Make Sure It Is Business First

Do not select a friend simply because you play tennis with her or enjoy a fun dinner together. She may be the right agent, but mixing friendship and business can be bad for both. You could lose a friend and lose money. Sometimes friends have a hard time telling other friends the true facts. They do not want to hurt the feelings of the other party. So time can be wasted, and time wasted is money lost. In every transaction, buying and selling a home should be business first and foremost.

Relocation Companies Establish the Benchmark

When a corporate executive is transferred, many companies seek the services of a top relocation company. They have understood for decades that broker qualifications and agent selection are the most important factors in real estate. Continuous monitoring of all activity is done by the relocation companies. The agents participating in these programs are held accountable at all levels of performance.

Relocation agents go through special training to become qualified to work with corporate executives. Relocation companies usually pick the top performing agents, but not all of them are willing to do what has to be done to satisfy the relocation department and the clients. What is this treatment and why is it not available to every buyer and seller? Relocation firms match the agent as closely as possible to the client. Top agents have highs and lows during their sales careers, just like baseball players. So if you are in the bottom of the ninth inning and the score is tied, you do not bring in a pinch hitter who has not had a hit in 24 times at bat, even if he hit .350 the preceding year. Neither do you want a top agent who is surrounded by wall plaques but has not had a sale in three months.

Manage Your Own Relocation

Matching buyers according to their financial needs, specific price range, and personality is done automatically in relocation circles. If the match does not pan out, the relocation company replaces the agent immediately. It is good business for all parties. Raise the expectations, raise the results. They know the value of client relationships and the agent is being managed by the relocation specialist and the local real estate office manager. Herein lies the key: the agent is being *managed.* Yes, managed. Most buyers and sellers do everything but manage the agent they are working with. Blaming them for lack of success is not managing them.

The best home search results come about when agent and buyer work as a team. An important part of managing effectively requires the ability to listen carefully to the facts and eliminate the emotional factors that can lead to bad decisions. So often real estate agents will say, "I told them what they needed to hear, but they didn't want to listen." Honesty is the best policy, but it may take some second effort to prove its worth. Your asset is at risk, and regardless of the effort; no one has more chips on the table than the buyer and the seller. Do not give up the reins of the horse you're riding or it just might take you in a direction you do not want to go.

How Do You Find a Top Agent?

There are many ways to go about doing this, but for the most part, the following method works the best. When getting ready to buy or sell, always contact at least two different offices in the area. Ask to speak with the manager. Make an appointment to visit with that manager in his or her office. Do not talk much on the phone. It is the first step in your evaluation of the office, the manager and the potential agent of choice. Describe what you want to accomplish. Be specific in your goals. Ask the manager to give you several choices of top agents to review. A personality match can help but knowledge and experience is what should be the driving forces for the match. After you have been given several choices, review their resumes and ask the manager to set up appointments for you to interview the potential agents.

Conduct an Interview

Keep in mind that you are getting ready to enter the real estate business and you are working with your own money. You have the right to select an agent that fits your needs. Years ago most of us went to the doctor and whatever they said, we took as gospel. Today most patients seek two or three opinions before doing anything. Apply this same thinking to your search for the right agent. Talk to several agents and you will know when you have the right one. The following questions will serve to open the doors to the skills of the agents you are talking with:

* *How long have you been selling real estate?*

* *Have you lived in the area very long?*

* *How many homes did you sell last year?*

* *Have you sold or listed many homes in the price range we are looking?*

* *How good of a negotiator are you? Can you provide some actual examples?*

* *Are you working with many buyers right now?*

* *When did you make your last sale and what price range was it in?*

※ *How many homes do you preview each week?*

※ *Do you actually go inside the homes during your previews?*

※ *How can the internet help us find a home?*

※ *What do you expect from us as buyers?*

※ *How long do you think it will take for us to find a home?*

※ *Are you available seven days a week?*

※ *How long have you been with this agency?*

※ *What are the technological advantages your company offers?*

※ *Are you strong in financial areas?*

※ *When problems come up after a contract is signed, what do you still consider your role to be?*

After spending time with an agent one of the best questions to ask yourself is this: "Would I buy a home from this person?" Somehow that clears the playing field and tells you what you want to know.

You do not have to ask all of these questions, but many of them will help you get a good feel for the background of the agent. Look for the right qualities to come through: if they are good at what they do, they will handle all of these questions professionally and with a positive attitude. They should also have the facts to backup their words. You can learn a lot about agents during the interview process, and the way they apply their skills.

Base Your Decision to Find the Best Agent on Proven Business Practices

To repeat: don't just sign up with the first agent you meet in the office, or with a person you know only as a social acquaintance. Seek the best professional with the help of the office manager. The manager's involvement will help keep the pressure on the agent to perform at his or her best. That is good for you and the agent. If the answers to all the questions seem right in line with your expectations and you like the agent, make your choice and let the home search begin on a positive footing. Always look for someone you can trust. High on the skills list should be the agent's ability to negotiate the best terms and conditions for you, the buyer. A strong work ethic is a must; viewing homes only on the internet, for example, is not going to score high marks in the plus column. You want an agent who will preview the homes on site and weed out the ones that do not fit your desires. Be honest with your agent. They are not magicians. They cannot change the marketplace but they can find and substantiate the best values that meet your needs. That has great value in itself.

Look for These Agent Qualifications

Local market knowledge, awareness of the current consumer protections, enthusiasm, strong negotiation skills, communication skills, honesty, trustworthiness, and a recent strong track record of sales are qualities you should look for in a good agent. Seek proof that the agent is a "realtor" or "realtor-associate" and therefore a member of the National Association of Realtors. In addition, seek an agent with a keen sense of urgency, a strong work ethic, creative marketing skills, a good understanding of finances, and the ability to work with others. Look for a genuine commitment to you as a customer. Integrity is a must. The sales agent needs to determine what the buyer can and cannot live without. The more honest you are about your true desires, the better the chances you will find your dream home. With broker selection complete now let's get "moving."

6 LET THE HOME SEARCH BEGIN

Keep a good sense of perspective when looking to find your home; there will be some good days and some bad days, too. Be prepared to respond quickly to any potential property. Getting there first can help; the early bird not only gets the "worm" but it just might get the rest of the property, too! Be ready to see a home at any hour and on any day. When the market is low in inventory your "buyer speed" has to increase accordingly. When all is said and done, the gain will more than outweigh the effort. Sometimes it takes a series of small moves before you are ready for that one big move.

Everything Is Relative

The more skilled you are at telling your agent what you want, the more likely he or she will be to find your home. Statements like "we want a large property" mean nothing unless you detail what a large property means to you. Is it 100' x 100' or is it 2 acres? What is a good-sized family room? If you never had one before a 12 x 10 room might seem huge. What is a quiet street? What do low taxes mean?

Everything is relative to the background and experiences of the individual providing the information. Describe what it means to you and qualify it as best you can with the agent. If you look at a home and the rooms are too small, that is good. The agent will now know exactly what you do not want and that helps them find what you do want. If you drive by a home or area that does appeal to you, even if it is not on the market, explain to your agent what caught your eye, whether it was the style, setting, or street location. This will save you and the agent valuable time in your home search.

Imagine calling a tailor and describing the suit you want. You enter the store and he walks you past hundreds of other suits. No one says anything. You walk into a room and there is the suit he wants to show you, resting on a hanger, all by itself. You look at it and tell him it is not what you wanted. You explain why and then both of you turn and walk out past hundreds of other suits. You never look at the other examples all around you. This sounds a lot like driving in a car for twenty minutes to view one house, while passing dozens of examples of other homes that might appeal to you. Use all of the market.

The Home Interview Can Help the Search

When you feel comfortable with your choice of agent, you might invite the agent back to see your home or apartment. He or she could learn a lot about your requirements by seeing first-hand your existing living space and furniture. Sometimes in the comfort of your own space you can reveal exactly what you are looking for in your next home.

Spending More Than You Can Afford?

Most people do not have the cash to buy a home

outright. If you need to borrow money to purchase a home, you will lose some control over your real estate purchase, but banks or lending institutions will not allow you to get in over your head. They will not lend you money if you cannot afford to make the payments, even if they think you are a nice person. If your credit is bad or you do not have enough income to carry the payments for taxes, principal, interest and insurance, you will not get the loan you applied for. Your enthusiasm for the home of your choice plays no part in the role of the other vendors involved in the transaction. They do what Joe Friday did best; they deal in the facts only.

Safety Valves Protect and Eliminate Fear

The fact that a lending institution can prevent you from becoming overextended on a mortgage should be viewed in a positive light, a "safety valve" that should eliminate any anxieties over whether you can really afford the home you want.

When purchasing a home, most buyers experience many of the same emotions they feel when they decide to get married, such as excitement, a feeling that dreams are about to come true, reasonable doubt at times, and the fear of the unknown. However, your contract will have many contingencies in it to protect your rights as a buyer. An attorney review is standard in most parts of the country. Home inspections, carpenter and termite inspections, environmental inspections and a mortgage contingency are all part of the normal buying process. All but the mortgage contingency are usually taken care of within fourteen days from the signing of the contract. In most cases the mortgage contingency is 30-45 days. The lender will verify your employment income and bonuses, assets, credit standing, outstanding debts, length of employment, and perform an independent appraisal of the home you wish to purchase. Many conditions need to be satisfied before you can take possession of a home.

Other protections can come in the form of home warranties, title insurance, homeowners insurance, and town-issued certificates of occupancy for new construction or homes that were seriously left unattended. All of these must come together for the lender to grant you the written mortgage commitment. If you do not qualify for the loan as stated in the contract, you will not be able to buy the house unless you increase your down payment to reach the contract price.

Today's buyers are fully protected by many consumer protection traditions in real estate. So relax and remember that the final decision to buy a home comes from a conservative group of business people. If they give you the "green light," you can move forward with confidence.

Consumer Protections Can Build Confidence

Consumer protection for home buyers has never been stronger. Years ago it was "caveat emptor," or buyer beware. In those days just about everything was tilted in the seller's favor. If you closed on the house and found out the seller had lied or not disclosed certain facts, it was just too bad. You owned it and that was that. For many years we have had a complete reversal of that position. It is now "seller beware." More recently, a written "sellers disclosure form" has been introduced and is used in addition to the factual listing of each property. This will be covered in more detail later. Today most buyers can feel confident that the purchase they make will come with great protections. Over the last few decades, consumer protection laws have helped residential home buyers be sure they get what they expected.

Real Estate Is Not a Science

Finding a home is like looking for a mate. If you described what you wanted, most of us would have something written on paper that is quite different from the person we ended up with. Like finding a mate, buying a home is a very emotional experience. There must be chemistry to make it work. Chemistry is almost impossible to put into words. When it happens, you know it, and when it does not, you also know it. Imagine how easy it would be to find a home if all you had to do was fill out one of those qualifying sheets that describes exactly what you want: amount of monthly payment; ideal distance to work; number of bedrooms and baths; etc. The agent would then just plug your requests into the office computer and out would come the home for you.

The problem with this scenario is that there's no substitute for actually seeing a possible home and experiencing the feeling that it's the right place for you. This cannot be quantified on any qualifying sheet. "Chemistry" can't be spit out of a computer.

Buyers Are Not "Liars"

There is no such thing as a "looker," that is, a person who looks at homes out of curiosity only. Every person who takes the time to look at a home has a reason for doing so. It may even seem to them that they are not ready at the time, but anything can happen. The largest oak tree started as a tiny seed. Quite often so-called "lookers" buy on the first day, and sellers who did not appear ready to sell list their homes after finding a house they love. If an agent believes the "looker" mentality, these clients will remain a low priority and the agent's efforts to work with them may be minimal. The agent may therefore be surprised to learn several months later that one of his "lookers" just closed on a home with someone else. The agent may feel betrayed or lied to, but in fact he probably should have given his so-called "looker" another "look."

Buyers are not liars, they are just people that are trying to educate themselves, and certainly have the right to change their minds during the process. As we gain more knowledge we start to prioritize our thinking, and as a result many things can change. Some buyers get educated in several days and others seem to stay in a deep rut, continuously looking for more information. If you are going nowhere with your home search, think about meeting with your agent and setting the record straight. Sometimes too much information can act as a "shield" from being able to "pull the trigger" on a decision. Keep in mind that the market does not wait for anyone. It just keeps rolling along like a giant river. However, once you get in that "river," you're secure, because the real estate "appreciation flow" is moving your home with the rest of the market. Sitting on the bank and throwing stones at the "real estate river" will not stop it. Continuing to rent will not stop it. Waiting for rates to come down will not stop it. Only supply and demand control the flow of the river.

Trade-Offs Are the Name of the Game

Buyers often make trade-offs to arrive at their final decisions. If you were to compare the information provided by buyers on their first day of viewing homes with their actual purchases, you would be amazed at the differences. You would find that quite often buyers end up with something completely different from what they said they initially wanted. How can this happen? You wanted a two-car garage but you end up with one. You wanted to be within 30 minutes of work and you ended up 45 minutes away. You wanted to spend $375,000 and you spent $400,000. Why? Trade-offs. Tastes do not change, and most of us do not like to settle for anything less that what we really want. Sure, you only got a one-car garage, but you ended up with the extra large master bedroom and bath. You wanted to be on a quiet street, but the house was on a large property and set back from the road. You wanted a large eat-in kitchen, but you ended up with a family room with a fireplace. Buyers make such trade-offs all the time. They are merely the means by which we prioritize our wants and needs.

Value Moves What a Buyer Will Spend, Not an Agent

When value presents itself, it is amazing how much deeper the pockets can become. In addition, there are some buyers who actually low-ball what they can afford because they fear their agent will try to sell them a house they cannot afford. As previously mentioned, there are safeguards to prevent this from happening. What can and usually does happen is that a buyer will see nothing in his price range, so his agent will propose moving "up the price ladder" a step to broaden the choices.

Agents cannot change your tastes, they can only find out what your desires are and then try to match them with the market values and your purchasing power. Value is the name of the game. Paying a lot and getting poor value is a very bad move. Paying less and getting poor value is a bad move. Paying fairly and getting fair value is good. Paying fairly and getting great value is best.

Make Your Offer Stand Out and Be Noticed

One day you get the call and off you go. You pull up to the house and your goose bumps have snow caps on them. You look at each other and silently you say, "this is it." As you walk up the steps you whisper these words, "try not to show too much enthusiasm or it will cost us in the offer." Or, you whisper "I love it" in such low tones that only the dog hears it. Sometimes it is only a glance that tells the story. If the chemistry is there, the buyer intensity increases. Sometimes thoughts are easier to control than body language.

As you walk through each room, you know this is it. You start to get a little light headed. You picture all your furniture in every room. You start to figure out who and what will go where. The opportunity train is stopping and you are ready to get on board. Your luggage is packed.

You start to ask the key buyer questions. What is the price again? How long has it been on the market? Have they had any offers? When do they want to close? How much of a mortgage would we need? What are the taxes? How close are the schools? Your furniture "flashes" in front of you and everything starts to come together like a giant puzzle. The realtor knows you are ready to make an offer and you know it, too. A strong gut feeling beckons you to make your move.

Timing Comes in Many Forms, But Bad Timing Is the Worst

When the moment of decision arrives, you must be ready to move with authority and determination. When our logical side and our emotional side see what they want, they can send a strong internal signal. It is that gut feeling that can provide the adrenalin to make it happen. Look for balance in your information, sources, and experience. Great timing is a result of knowledge, preparation and execution, all playing on the same team with a common goal. Luck plays no part in real estate. I have seen people that were offered a fabulous opportunity find reasons not to proceed. That "if" list appears real quickly for some buyers. Remember, that "Opportunity Train" will come by, open the door and leave, with or without you. Timing is critical when the opportunity is right. Rarely do those gut feelings mislead you. If you do not want to trust others, trust yourself.

Review the Seller's Disclosure Form Before Making an Offer

As mentioned, years ago there was a true "buyer beware" mentality in real estate. Regardless of what went wrong, the seller was off the hook. Buyer beware has now been replaced with seller beware, however, and the principal instrument responsible for this is the "seller disclosure form," used throughout most of the country. Upon listing a home, sellers must disclose any known defects or trouble areas in the home. This includes any known future assessment notices they may have received in writing. Even years after a sale has closed, a buyer can come back at a seller, if they were in fact lied to, or fraud was committed by the owner. Never before has seller disclosure been so required. Knowing what you are buying is always better than getting a bad surprise. Some homes are sold "as is;" that is, the seller is making no guarantees and the house has to be taken as is. If that is the upfront position, then the buyer knows exactly what to expect. However, even "as is" homes may be subject to certain legal requirements by state and local authorities.

Always review the seller disclosure prior to making any offer. It will help avoid any big surprises and also serve as a reminder of any potential trouble areas.

The Cool Breeze of Fear

You feel yourself getting a bit overheated. You know the decision is coming and coming soon. Then you start to feel the reality of the move and the enormity of the change. You just want to let everything remain "status quo." Change is not easy. Progress does not come without apprehension. Sometimes the "what ifs" start to enter your vocabulary and you feel yourself cooling off. The "fear breeze" is blowing and your feet are turning blue. You talk about making a low-ball offer, one that you know will not get accepted. You get defensive about what the seller wants. Anything to get home and pull those blankets over your head!

You want to put the decision off. You want to wait until

tomorrow. You need time. Stop. Take a deep breath. Build your confidence. You are prepared. You know what you can pay. You know what you want. You know values. You know that others will help determine if you can buy the home. Consumer protection is on your side. You know a conservative institution will ultimately decide if you can get the loan. That same institution will appraise the house before lending you the money. Remember in the long run, you want the "place," not second place. At times our fears may be like bandits that snatch our confidence and limit our actions but overcoming fear is like winning the lottery and not having to pay taxes!

Verbal Offers Work Against You

When you have found the home you want, you will ask many questions, and based upon the answers and your mental readiness, you may want to make an offer. If so, always make it in writing. Verbal offers allow the seller to hear only the price and not the whole story of you as a buyer. Smart sellers will not respond to a verbal offer. They will simply request that you put it in writing. Quality real estate agents will not present verbal offers for these reasons. Verbal offers are not in your best interests, period. Sometimes requesting a written offer is enough to avoid a so-so attempt at an offer, one filled with indecision and apprehension that it might actually be accepted. If a buyer is not serious enough to make a written offer, then she should continue looking at homes until she finds one she's serious about purchasing. There are many people who would argue this point, claiming they purchased their house based on a verbal offer. Maybe so, but did they get as good a deal as they could have if the offer was in writing?

Price Is Not the Only Factor That Counts

Initially, price seems to be the only thing that matters in making an offer on a home. However, other terms are very important, too. Your strength as a buyer is a critical negotiating point. Your ease in getting a mortgage, for example, is a strong card in any deal. Not having a home to sell or including a contingency for the sale of a property is a huge positive for any seller. The closing date can be a determining factor, too, because it represents time and money. If you want to close in eight months and the seller wants to close in 90 days, the deal might not go, even at full price. If you have a high offer but the amount of the down payment is less than 10%, you may appear to be in a weak position to some sellers. The number and type of contingencies included in the contract also can make a difference. Standard contingencies include home inspections, attorney reviews, termite and carpenter inspections, radon inspections and other environmental issues. Special contingencies involving zoning approvals should be looked at carefully from both sides. Offers with contingencies for subdivisions must be studied carefully and weighed against offers without that contingency.

A fair offer and reasonable terms and conditions will show the seller that you are serious about closing on time. It is the buyer's determination to close the transaction that will take you to the closing table, not just the agreed-upon price.

Number of Days on the Market Is a "Must Know" for the Buyer

The market is the ultimate judge of price. Appraisers

do not buy real estate. They express opinions. Furthermore, experts in every field seldom agree on much. Real estate is not a science. What happens one day might not happen the next. If five homes came on the market on your street, the market would change that day. However, nothing tells the truth better about market conditions than the number of days a house is on the market. If it sells the first day or first month, value was there in the mind of the buyer. Conversely, if a property has been on the market for thirty days, momentum builds in the favor of the buyer making a lower offer than the asking price.

The simple rule of thumb to follow is that the shorter the time period the home has been on the market, the less flexible the seller will be. Even if the property is overpriced most sellers will not recognize that during the first few weeks. Sellers will often turn down a good offer made the first week their property is listed, only to see that price never offered again. The longer a property is on the market, the more negotiating room the buyer will have. When a home stays on the market, home history is building each day. How many showings? How many written offers? Broker feed back. Buyer feed back. Its market history is now fact, not speculation.

Make an Offer That Doesn't Scare Off the Seller

Generally speaking, buyers do not make written offers on homes they do not want to own. When you consider what to offer, ask yourself this question. At the full price, is this house one of the best values I have seen? It is value that is in question here. Some buyers know they have a great deal and yet insist on making a low offer. They get hung up on the competitive part of negotiating. Oftentimes, they lose the house and regret it. If you do not like the home enough to want to live there, it won't matter what the price is (unless you are an investor). Most buyers know what they want when they see it and if they understand value and the market, they are in the best of positions.

If you like the home and want to buy it, be determined to get it. Make a fair offer and make your offer as strong as you can. In many parts of the country the market has been so hot that multiple offers come in on many homes. When this occurs, an "auction" atmosphere is created and the seller is in a great position to pick and choose the best offer. In more than a few instances, the home ends up selling for more than the listed price. Supply and demand are two strong forces.

Sellers Establish Price, But Buyers Determine Value

If you find yourself in a position where yours is one of several offers on a property, it is good in at least one respect: you have excellent proof of the home's value in today's market. When you decide to sell this home, that strong market appeal should still be there. You may pay more than the seller is asking, but you are probably getting more value than most homes offered at the same price. Multiple offers affirm your evaluation of the property.

Once you know you have a good house and a solid value, it is time to make that offer. Do not go home to think it over unless you're having second thoughts. This is a critical point. If you have legitimate concerns, wait it out. But if you are certain the home is right, put your fears aside and move quickly to get it.

Value Is What Is Important, Not Just Price

If you saw a house for $450,000 and could buy it for $375,000, that does not necessarily mean you got a good value. If you paid $475,000 for a house listed at $450,000, that doesn't necessarily mean that you overpaid for the home. The point here is that price is only one factor, and how it is determined is always an inexact science. The fact of the matter is that some realtors go through the process of establishing comparative values for a listing presentation, but often end up listing the home at the price the sellers insist upon. That price may or may not be in line with the market.

What you get for your money is what counts the most. If you are an educated buyer and are aware of recent comparable sales, you are ready to find good value. A good general observation to keep in mind is that the higher the price range, the harder it is to determine specific value. A 5% variance in appraisals on a $2,000,000 dollar house is $100,000, whereas on a $400,000 house it's only $20,000. Quite the difference.

What Do I Offer?

If the number of days on the market is less than thirty, be prepared to hit some stiff resistance to an offer less than 95% of the asking price. If the home has been on for several months you may have a strong advantage as a buyer. The market is writing the history of this property. Opinions are no longer valid. Market days and activity rule. They tell the truth. Rely on them strongly. Since many condominiums in a condo complex are similar in layout and amenities, ask your broker to show you the most recent "sold" prices before you make an offer. This may not work as well in other single family residential areas, but where there are cluster homes (in a planned community, for example), it can be very significant because of similar comparables.

If the value is there, make a strong offer to get the home. Coming in second is never fun. One successful approach is to work with percentages as a means of making an offer. An offer of 95% of the asking price is a good place to start. On a $500,000 house that would be $475,000. Presentation matters. Stating that you are offering "95% of the asking price" sounds better than saying that you want the house for $25,000 less than the seller's price. Who would not listen to an offer that gave them 95% of what they were looking for? It works! Currently, few, if any, agents use this method, but it is effective when presented properly. It will stick in the sellers mind. Today even the stock market reports everything in terms of percentages and not just dollars.

Earnest Money Can Make Your Offer Stand Out

Years ago you could make an offer with a mere $100 deposit. Today, most of the time, an offer is accompanied by a check from the buyer for anywhere from $500 to $5,000. In most cases, I would encourage a buyer to make a large earnest money deposit with an offer. This will allow a realtor to present you as a serious purchaser. Writing a check of considerable size will get the attention of both the broker and the seller. In reality, earnest money does not go to the seller but is held in "escrow" by the broker or a legal representative; if the offer is not accepted, the money is returned to the buyer. If an agreement is signed, the initial deposit money is held in trust, along with an additional deposit, usually required within ten days of the execution of the formal contracts. The two deposits generally total between 5% and 10% of the sales price. No money is released until all contingencies are met and satisfied, regardless of who holds the money in trust. In many cases the deposit monies are held in trust until the closing of title.

Humanize the Buyer and Present the People, Not Just the Contract

When the offer is ready to be presented it is important that the party making the presentation humanizes the buyer. Be sure you or the agent presenting the offer tells the seller how much you love the home. If it is suitable, compliment the owner on the decorating and the care shown by the home owner. You can get a lot more sellers to the closing table with honey that you can with lemons.

Some people say you should not do this because it weakens your position. That may be true in some business or investment deals, but we are talking about a highly sensitive degree of seller pride. In most cases, complimenting the seller helps the seller respond to your offer without animosity. There have been thousands of examples where the fact that the seller personally liked the buyer helped in the negotiation. Remember, if you touch the seller's "pride button" in the wrong way, it just might turn off the deal or cost you even more money. This is not the time to be unpleasant or hostile in your negotiations.

Avoid Multiple Counter Offers

Many a great house has been lost because the buyer and seller forgot about the objective. Make a fair offer the first time. Do not insult the seller if the house has been on the market for only a few weeks. Sellers can react very strongly and actually counter even higher than they might have if your offer had been fair and strong. Please keep in mind that all negotiating terms should start with your perception of the value of the property. If the fair market value is not clear, then the number of days on the market does not matter. Just because a home has only been on the market for a short period of time does not mean it represents a good value. Many homes come on the market overpriced. However, the seller is usually not ready to accept an offer that is not close to the asking price early in the game. In this case, you just might wait it out a bit.

When the seller comes back to you with a counter offer, make every attempt to close the deal with your next response. Look to compromise and allow the seller to feel like they "got something," too. Believe it or not, the ego and the emotional tug of war during negotiations can cause sane people to react in some pretty crazy ways. Stay focused on the main issues and work toward a fair settlement of price and terms. Do not deliver offers with ultimatums or threats. When that occurs the emotions have clearly gotten out of control. The competitive juices are just flowing too hard. When a buyer and seller start to compete just to get the better of the other a good deal can go bad.

Perform According to the Contract

Once the terms and conditions have been agreed upon and a formal contract has been signed by all parties, perform accordingly.

Do what you are expected to do, and do it on time. During strong seller markets there just might be another buyer hanging in the background waiting for an opportunity to jump in to the action. You do not want to open that door. Move quickly with your attorney and/or escrow companies. Keep in mind that many states do not use attorneys to close title. Escrow companies often perform the necessary functions needed for a closing of title. Get all contingencies met according to the contract. If more time is needed, get it in writing. Nothing verbal has much meaning if challenged, unless it is witnessed by a crowd, but even then opinions can vary far too much to have any real value.

Do not assume that every professional involved in the transaction will do all they are supposed to do. Most of the time it all works just fine, but stay on top of things. Participate in the process and do not stick your head in the sand. The stakes are high and the buyer and seller have the most to gain or lose. Hang on to the reins.

Swiss Cheese Can Teach Us a Lot

Look at a piece of Swiss cheese. Do you see the holes or the cheese? Most of us have heard the one about the glass. Is it half full or half empty? It all depends on what's in the glass—if it's filled with gold, just about everyone will see it as half full.

I like to think of a piece of Swiss cheese as a blueprint

to getting you where you want to go. You can navigate the field if you know where the holes are and how to avoid falling into them. Real estate is a tangible business and most times you can see where you want to go. Legal protections for the buyer are strong and will help keep you away from the holes.

Naturally, problems do arise, but the majority of them can be fixed if you stay focused and are determined to find a fair solution. This is where having a knowledgeable third party really pays off. He or she will fight for you to find fair and equitable solutions. Nothing helps a deal close on time more than a willing buyer, a willing seller, and a willing agent.

Holding Vendors Accountable

As I mentioned earlier, it is important to stay engaged in the transaction. If you sense something is not going according to plan or someone is not doing his job, demand action and answers. The longer the deal stays in limbo the greater the chance it will fall through. If the desire or willingness to close escapes either the buyer or seller, you're headed for the loss column.

Even when highly intelligent people transact real estate, they can make some big mistakes. When they sell their own home or buy a new one they often leave their business talents behind and deal from emotion only. Lawyers, home inspectors, brokers, and friends all may participate in the process but the buyer and seller are the only ones fully committed to changing ownership. Like the story about ham and eggs, the participants differ greatly in their level of commitment. The chicken was "involved" in the process but the pig was "committed."

Most of the people helping to sell your home work for you. Manage them. When you go to the closing, it is your check book that is providing the payroll.

7 HOME IMPROVEMENT

Increasing your equity by developing the raw potential of a home can bring enormous dividends. That "savings and loan" you create with equity growth will be ready to produce profits almost immediately. You can improve the outside with landscaping and paint. Throw in a few stone walls, a brick walk, and a great patio, and you have increased the value substantially. Why? Appeal factor. Sometimes simply changing the color of a house, adding window boxes with flowers, or new shutters can increase "curb appeal" enormously.

Remember, although a dress may cost $350, without the make up, perfume and accessories, maximum appeal can never be realized. Homes need to be dressed up and accessorized too.

Some buyers cannot or do not want to see past a good coat of dust. They would rather buy new and clean even if the basic construction was not that good. Bad move. Years later the construction will show up poorly, and if the location was not great to begin with the house is not going to be easy to sell. Poor construction leads to high maintenance costs. If you are inclined to do the maintenance work yourself, talk to tradesmen who have knowledge in the area you need help with. Good home improvement stores often have retired carpenters or painters with whom you can get advice. Do not be afraid to bite off a bit more than you can chew. That is how you learn, build confidence and reap the rewards. Know your limitations, but understand that a handy person can save thousands on improvements. It's also great physical exercise and can give you a great sense of accomplishment. For many "sweat equity" is no sweat! Home improvement and self improvement make a great team.

What Improvements Pay Off the Most?

It is old news to say improvements in bathrooms, kitchens, master bedrooms and family rooms pay off the most. What pays off the most is actually buying a good home in an A+ neighborhood. There will always be someone looking for the best. For years we have been told by the experts that you shouldn't over-improve a home beyond its street value. In certain markets where the land supply has run out this statement may no longer be true. Older streets will turn over eventually, and homeowners will make large additions and other substantial improvements. Sure enough, the street values will go up again, especially in a strong seller market and where the lots are big and zoning permits a large home "footprint."

Hard Work and Common Sense Can Bring Uncommon Dollars

The first home I ever owned had been condemned by the town. It was built in 1806, when Thomas Jefferson was President. I am sure he had no idea I would be buying it in 1968. It was vacant for three years, and the property was completely over grown. Only about 30% of it showed from the road. It sat on one acre of property and the gardens that once were spectacular were all but gone. The buffalo grass in the front yard hid the lower windows. A huge pine tree covered the rest of the house. A raccoon had gotten into the basement and somehow short-circuited the heating unit. The home had suffered severe water damage when the water pipes broke during a cold winter. The ceilings had all fallen down from the water damage and plaster, horsehair, and lathing strips were everywhere. The pipes had frozen and the bathrooms were filled with pieces of broken porcelain. The place looked like it was about to fall over for the last time. But we loved it!

When we left the closing we had $19 in total cash savings left. We were expecting our first child and I was working three jobs. Still, at the time buying this home seemed the only thing to do. But it took commitment, a sense of adventure, and courage to take on a project like that.

Life Tests Us All

One night just after we closed I came home and was informed that the washing machine had broken. We had inherited the washer and dryer with the house. They were 15 years old at the time, but they still worked when we bought the place, and we could not afford new ones. I was teaching, refinishing antiques for a local dealer, and running a small house painting business. In my spare time I worked every night until midnight on the house. On weekends, the work schedule was about fifteen hours a day. I was tired and my emotions were a little raw, but nonetheless, after dinner I went under that washing machine and started poking around. Looking up at a small plastic housing, it appeared to be the problem. It was, and I found out the "wet way." It broke. The entire washload of water, soap, and who knows what came down on me. There was only one thing to do for a man of courage, determination, and uncanny handyman skills. I went outside and shed a few tears.

It was the lowest moment of my life up to that point. It was a true crossroad. Then I looked up and realized the sun was still out. We had a baby on the way and all of this was going to pass. I ordered the part and in a few days we were back in business. I learned that day what others in our great country have known for years: never, never, give up on something you believe in. I believed in real estate. I believed in the restoration of that great antique home and that was that.

We worked on the home for seven years. We did every room over. My wife was the decorator and I was the carpenter, plumber, electrician, mason, painter, landscaper, and caretaker. It took old fashion "stick-to-itive-ness" to make this work. For a time, we lived in an 8 x 10' bedroom with a drop cloth over the door. I remember taking twenty-four wheelbarrows of plaster and debris from the living room alone. Some adventure!

What we saw was a "great set of bones" on a large property in one of the best towns around. The home had two fireplaces, four bedrooms, two baths, a first floor laundry room, and a nice sized kitchen. It also had a two car detached garage. The home had much more than we could have ever afforded if it had been in normal condition.

It turned out to be a showplace and the stories of its reconstruction are still told in that town. "American ingenuity" they called it in the magazine article. It was a team effort that paid off with a home larger than we could have ever dreamed and enough "sweat equity" to fill a gymnasium.

We sold the home for almost four times what we paid for it. Common sense, hard work, courage, and good old fashion ingenuity had worked. We never could have saved the money we made on that house, in any other way, even if we had each worked three jobs.

Parting Thoughts

Home ownership is one of the greatest freedoms that we enjoy. Our government provides more individual tax advantages for home ownership than most any other tax-related program. Because most people only live in a home for an average of seven years, statistically, at least, you will have many opportunities during your lifetime to "make the right moves in real estate." Your experience and knowledge from one transaction will help you with the next.

There is an old saying that's apropos of just about any transaction: buying is a lot easier than selling. Keep in mind that nothing helps the selling process more than "buying right."

8 SELLING YOUR HOME

The Tug of War That Determines Decisions

After seven years of working on the restoration of that old farm house, the time had come to move on to another challenge. The home was great in many ways but with a growing family our needs were changing and we were ready to move.

The farmhouse had become a very important part of our family unit. We loved it and it meant a great deal to us. Yes, we had put far more of ourselves into that place than most people do. Nonetheless, it was time for change. It was not an easy decision. We had talked about moving many times. Perhaps part of it was that we had done all we wanted to do on this house and we were up for another challenge. Then one day we heard about a great house that was on the market. We went to see it just for the "heck of it." My wife and I had not spent ten minutes there when we both knew that this was the "one." It was in the same town, on a cul-de-sac and only ten years old. The tug of war between moving and staying had begun. You see, we were just "lookers" but we found what we wanted unexpectedly. It did not take long for the tug of war to end. For others the decision to move can go back and forth for days, weeks and even years.

Within hours we had made an offer on the home. We knew in our gut that we were doing the right thing at the right time. Knowledge, determination, and courage trumped any anxiety we have had about making a move.

I honestly think the emotions of buying and selling are at opposite ends of the spectrum. When you are buying a home you are filled with dreams, anticipation, and excitement. When you go to sell your house you are filled with the fear of change, the worry of spending too much money, and the hope that your home sale will generate all the dollars you expect. In addition, many home owners can feel quite low emotionally about leaving a place that held so many good memories. It is tough to move out of the "comfort zone." Buying and selling real estate can put you on an emotional roller coaster. For that reason alone, many of the most intelligent people in the world may not handle the sale of their personal residence as well as they do all their other business transactions.

Seller Emotions Can Surface

At the time of this purchase I had just entered the real estate business and was having great success. My income was rising and so were our needs and desires. I did not know a lot about real estate at that time but after a successful teaching career, I certainly knew a lot about people. I also knew that I loved home ownership and the feeling of pride that comes from working hard and having something to show for it.

Our farmhouse was appraised and placed on the MLS for sale. Finding an agent was not an issue because I was in the business.

The new purchase did represent a very large increase in our monthly payments, about three times what we were paying per month at the time. After seven years of working on an old home, the idea of having an almost new home was also very exciting. To this day I cannot get over the fact that you can actually open a window without the need of a putty knife!

I can still see the smile on my office manager's face when I told him what took place. He knew I would do whatever I had to to make those payments. He was right, because it was not long before I became the number one sales person in a company with 100 sales agents. However, I had no idea that I would become that successful when we made the decision to buy. It occurred because my responsibilities had expanded. When you bite off more than you can chew, you learn to chew faster.

Everything was moving forward but I could feel that cool breeze of anxiety starting to blow. My stomach seemed to have a mind of its own and most of the time, it was nervous. We were anxious to sell and eliminate the burden of owning two homes.

Shortly, however, we received an offer on the farmhouse. A broker had called and said she wanted to come over and present it. My stomach started to feel better. Relief was on the way.

The Arrow Hits Us Where It Hurts the Most

I can remember that night like it happened yesterday. The agent arrived, but did not say anything nice about our house. She was one of the few people to enter our home and not be amazed by its historical beauty. It hurt a bit, but after all, she was not buying the home, just presenting an offer.

She started with some small talk. We were nervous and I could not help but try to see what the figure was on the top of the contract. I was just inches away from knowing that price; the minutes passed like days.

The agent began to tell us that although we had done a lot to the home, it still was an old house and needed more improvements. These were costs that the buyer would have to bear. Obviously she was building her case for a lower offer. I remember looking at my wife's face and seeing the anger building. Mount Rushmore had nothing on that stoney look. I felt the anger too. Who was she to be insulting our home? We had worked for seven years to restore a wonderful antique. It sent our body language backwards. But frankly, I wanted to get the home sold and find out what a good nights sleep felt like again. Then it happened. The arrow was out of the quiver. It was in the bow. The anticipation was awesome! It headed for its target. The price was on its way! It hit!

The offer was about $4,000 less than our asking price. I loved it. I knew at that moment it could be a deal. Unfortunately, my wife was not over the other arrow that had left the bow ten minutes earlier, the one that downgraded our home and told us that after all our work the buyer was still critical of our dream house. That arrow hit us in the heart, not the pocketbook. My wife stood up and said, "No way will we ever take that offer. We want full price and that is that." I felt the same logically, as anxious as I was to get the place sold. As it happens, the buyers wanted the house enough that they came up in price.

But in many similar cases the deal can be lost because of the lack of empathy for the sellers. Feelings are to be respected, regardless of the business issues. Hurt them and it might cost you a house.

Lessons Learned When the Stakes Are Highest Seem to Stick the Best

That incident taught me first hand what not to do when you present an offer. To this day I still have a bad feeling for that agent. It stuck with me. Since that experience, I have always favored preparing a seller for the offer by humanizing the buyer and complimenting the seller whenever appropriate. If the buyer or the agent presenting the offer pushes enough bad buttons, the seller can hit the off button—game over. Follow this advice: "Do unto others as you would have them to do unto you." Familiar yes, but not practiced nearly often enough anymore.

The love for a home can grow slowly over the years, and although the purchase of a new residence can be very exciting, leaving the old homestead can be difficult. When you execute a closing of title, you own a house. When you live in it for years, it becomes your home. When you experience good times and build lifetime memories, a home can become an integral part of your life.

To Sell or Not to Sell? That Is the Question

For most of us, the decision to sell a home works

something like a boomerang. We talk about moving from time to time, finding that "dream" house and adding some desired amenities. Then that discussion seems to just head out the window for awhile, only to return again. We continue to visit our friends' homes and see special rooms and styles that appeal to us. Everyone likes to dream a little. After awhile your rooms seem to get smaller as the kids get bigger. Somehow it even seems your furniture is growing overnight. Everything seems crowded. Keep that window open because that boomerang is coming back!

Some owners decide to improve their home instead of moving. It may show up first as decorating efforts, and later it might even include a few additions. For some, this may last for a few years or longer but it is amazing how many people end up moving shortly after making improvements on their home.

Move Motivators

There are lots of reasons people decide to move. Need more space. Need less space. Do not like the house anymore. Disputes with neighbors. Desire for a better school system is a big reason many buyers decide to pack. Changes in the town, death, divorce, illness, increased or decreased family size, and employment changes can cause strong market movement. Tired of an old house and want a new one. Tired of a new one and want an old one. Life changes, we change. Events make us change. Life is not stagnant.

Changes in income either up or down can create reasons to move. Still others are seeking certain creature comforts like an in-ground pool or a large modern kitchen. Some seek status, more land, and the privacy large properties can provide. Sometimes just the stimulation of "new and different" is a good enough reason to move.

DECISION MADE:
HOME CLEARED FOR TAKE-OFF

9

Once the decision to sell a home is made there are options to consider. One of the first decisions is whether or not to sell the home on your own or to list it with a real estate company. There have been successful and unsuccessful sales made by both methods.

It is important to remember that for most people a real estate transaction is the biggest financial transaction he or she will probably ever make. Use your own business logic in making decisions. Do not let your emotions alone run the show. The real estate transactions that usually turn out the worst are the ones where sellers and buyers are at an emotional pique. Staking a strong emotional position has a tendency to block out the problem solvers like logic, reason, and compromise.

Be realistic in your assessments. Buying and selling requires constant focus. Time is critical in most situations. Decisions have to be made and executed according to a well thought-out plan.

FSBO (For Sale By Owner)?
Or FSBB (For Sale By Broker)?

Just about everyone considers these two options. Even active real estate agents go through this mental exercise. Some have been known to try and sell their own house as a FSBO. A few real estate agents may feel that they know the business, knowledge which they believe separates them from most home owners. I disagree with that view and am reminded of the old aphorism, "When an attorney represents himself, he has a fool for a client." The fact remains that the market presents the same opportunities for all home owners, regardless of their career status. Sellers have the choice of going it alone, working with an agent, or choosing a combination of both.

Nationally speaking about 90% of all residential homes are sold by real estate companies. A certain percentage of those sellers probably first tried to sell their home on their own. Having no success or simply getting tired of trying to act as their own agent, they listed their property with a real estate company and went to a closing.

There is a lot to be learned from these figures. If it was so easy to sell on your own, then why do 90% of the sellers choose to place their home in the hands of the professionals? After all, if houses sold themselves, then why is anyone else necessary? The answer to these questions is simple: houses only sell themselves if the right qualified buyers are shown the properties, and the parties involved are able to successfully negotiate a fair and meaningful transaction. Therein lies most of the explanation for that 90% figure.

Real estate is not a science, so when you mix what appear to be the same ingredients, the results do not always come out the same. Anything can happen in a one-out ball game. A single sale of a home at a particular price should not set the bar for all other homes. In the real estate market activity is happening all the time. A seller could sell their home on their own and if the deal falls through, not get that same price again. The same thing can happen if it was listed with a broker. It's not an easy business. The number one reason why some sellers end up listing with a realtor, however, is the seller's inability to accept full responsibility for the sale and the building pressure that continues to mount if the home does not sell.

Sometimes There Is Not Enough "Fizz" in the FSBO

One day Mary and Bill decide to sell their home. They know several agents but question why they should pay a commission when they have a great house and the cost of a few ads will be nothing compared to paying thousands of dollars in fees. "We can save a lot of money and we will need every nickel for the new house." This sounds simple enough.

With the decision made to go FSBO, sellers have to make a few other decisions themselves. Where do we advertise the house? Do we want to place a sign in the front of the home? Do we want to give out our address to anyone who calls? What do we have to do to get the house ready to sell? Who will handle the negotiations? Do we list our home on the internet? Will we be home enough to make the house available for showings? How do we protect ourselves from strangers coming into our home and having our phone number and address? What price should we ask? Not overwhelming issues, but a sizeable basket of responsibilities.

Generally speaking, most sellers call in a few realtors to

get a competitive market analysis (CMA) on their home and to pick up some good pointers from the agents. Realtors provide this service for free and are not paid for their time and effort in making a listing presentation.

Sellers may also use information gathered from comparable neighborhood sales. As noted previously, this can be flawed. Checking out prices by looking at the newspaper or the internet can be very dangerous, too. When you see a house similar to yours and on the market for a specific price, it is natural to assume that the house will actually sell for that price. That is a false assumption. Only sold homes work to establish price values, not pretty pictures in the newspaper or on the internet. Like the "love match" networks on the internet today, what you see is not always what you get. Houses, like people, require more than a picture and a description to be fully evaluated and appreciated. The pictures or video "tours" of homes have been taken to present the strengths of a home, not the weaknesses. They can help, but when it comes to real estate, the bloom may be off the rose when you actually visit the property.

Buyers Target So-Called "Savings"

Usually a combination of data is sufficient for a seller to be able to price his or her home. If an agent suggests a listing price of $425, 000, which includes a commission, a FSBO seller will generally use that same price when listing a home on his or her own. The thinking is that the seller is "saving" the commission.

As far as a potential buyer is concerned, however, the FSBO price should be discounted by the amount of the absent commission. Of course, this line of reasoning does not occur when a buyer sees a home on the MLS. with a real estate company. When the buyer of a FSBO property is ready to make an offer, he or she will focus on the commission first. This usually results in the so-called seller "savings" being cut in half. The buyer quickly figures that is the only fair way to go. I have yet to hear a different approach from any buyer seeking to purchase a FSBO. The commission savings for the seller always becomes the first target for the buyer.

Shifting the Responsibility and Easing The Pressure

When an owner places his or her home on the market directly, the seller is subject to many of the same pressures and frustrations that real estate agents experience every day. Buyers can come through a house and say nothing at all. You can also have buyers who rave about a home, ask all the right buyer questions, and leave everyone with expectations soaring. You wait to hear something only to never hear from that buyer again. That hurts.

A FSBO seller can field many inquiries and spend hours preparing for appointments that somehow seem to vaporize. Even worse, some buyers just drive by houses without asking to come inside for a look. That can happen quite often when you give out information to strangers and have no control of the situation. It is very frustrating for a homeowner to look out the window at a prospective buyer sitting in the car looking at your home. As the seller, you want to run outside and start telling this buyer about your house. When the buyer pulls away, you can feel pretty disappointed. This may be particularly true if you have a home that doesn't do it justice from the curb side view. How do you get them inside to see all that your home offers?

You can also start to feel housebound. Your home starts to feel like an anchor. You do not like to go out and miss the chance of a buyer calling or wanting to come over for a viewing. Expectations go up and down like an elevator. Frustration begins to build. The pressure to sell continues to grow with each passing day. Fear of being caught between two homes starts to rise like a cake in the oven. Emotions get raw.

Human Nature Is Not Always So Human

Sometimes friends do not help the situation, either. They keep asking the same questions: "Is the house sold yet? Have you had any offers?" Or they continue to tell you about other homes that came on the market and did sell. That really hurts. Perhaps human nature is not so human at times. When you have to answer "no" to one of those questions, you feel just a little more rejected. And that is not a good feeling for most of us. All in all, friends may mean well but sometimes it is the part that hurts that sticks. For FSBO sellers costs can mount up on the advertising side, and although they may not be significant, they still require a check to be written. Finally, there is no one to blame for the house not selling. It has just become too personal of a matter. Pressure continues to build and finally the "escape door" opens to your local realtor. This is another main reason why 90% of homes are sold by real estate companies. Call it "FSBO Fatigue."

Now if the home is not selling or the activity is slow, the owner can shift the emotional responsibility to a third party. The goal of selling a home hasn't changed, but the responsibility for getting it done has. Help is on the way. Can you imagine if you did not have this option?

Use the Power of Networks to Spread the Word

In order to understand a basic principle of marketing, consider the networking power of hundreds of realtors having the information on your listing, compared to just the people who read the local paper, see your home on the internet, or happen to ride down the street and view the "For Sale By Owner" sign. Every agent has a list of active customers they contact when a home comes on the market. The best agents work by business referrals only. Clients seek them out. They do not spend time waiting for the phone to ring. They are prospecting everyday. That realtor network is huge and no single effort by anyone can compare to the potential qualified buyers captured by millions of dollars of advertising spent over many years. This is another reason that 90% of the homes in this country end up being sold by real estate agents.

Take the 10 to 100 Test

Consider this when selling your home. If you had a chance to sell a single item by showing it to ten people at $5 or showing it to a hundred people at $8, where would you place your bet as to the where the sale would occur? I think the answer is obvious. In that group of one hundred buyers, the chances of someone needing and wanting that item are huge compared to the smaller group. The number and quality of buyers For Sale By Owners reach compared to the Multiple Listing Service is significantly less. It is true you only need one buyer to make the sale happen, but sometimes you have to go through dozens of them to find the right qualified buyer.

On Other Hand, 10% of FSBOs Are Successful

There is no doubt that a homeowner can sell a property on his or her own successfully. Sometimes the stronger the market conditions for the seller, the better their chances. If the seller follows all the right procedures, is realistic about pricing, prepares the home properly, and stays focused on the issues at hand, it can and has been done many times.

If a homeowner can sell a house with a local ad and a sign on the front lawn, could he or she have sold the house for more money on the Multiple Listing Service? It seems logical to assume that due to the extensive marketing and customer base contained within the local realtor network, the homeowner could sell his or her home for enough money to cover the so-called commission "savings." In addition, when we add in the power of third party negotiations, the commission may well be totally absorbed right there. I have seen many transactions come together because of the value associated with third party negotiating skills. Remember saving five or six percent of nothing is nothing! Going head to head as a buyer and seller can cause some pretty severe head aches!

During very strong seller markets a self-initiated auction can help sell a home for even more than the listing price. This happens when a number of buyers want the same property and end up being told to submit their best bid for the house. All the bids are usually reviewed by the broker, the seller, and the seller's attorney, if desirable.

Are Agents Overpaid?

Most active agents make many listing presentations throughout a business year. In addition, they educate many buyers during the buying process. The average agent can drive over 25,000 miles a year showing homes and performing general business functions. This is worthy of note because the only time a real estate agent gets paid is when the title to a property closes legally. Yes, they are paid well on that particular day, but on all the other days, there is no pay at all.

Knowing this fact should help to keep in perspective the risk versus reward scenario. For the most part, real estate agents are not salaried employees. They are independent contractors and the risk is always there for no income at all. One thing is constant: expenses. Over the years some sellers and other vendors associated with real estate have felt that agents are overpaid for what they do. One reason for that line of thinking is that in many circumstances the only time some people see an agent is when a transaction closes and the commissions are paid. From that perspective it may look like an easy job. I'm sure that if every agent who knew an attorney or other related vendors called them each time he or she worked ten hours and made nothing, there would be a far better understanding of what an agent really earns.

In addition, when a fee is earned, it is divided at least four ways. For example, if the total commission is $20,000, the listing broker will usually get $10,000 and the selling broker $10,000. There may be a deduction for some listing fees, but for the most part the amount received by the brokers on either side of the transaction is then split again between the broker and the agent. In this case the selling agent would probably receive $5,000 for the transaction and the listing agent the same amount. Most companies scale up the portion for the agent as their production grows. In some cases referral fees are also paid to another company from the listing or selling portion, further reducing the amount paid to the company and agent.

Think of reversing how most people view a commission. Think of it as a professional fee that can in reality actually save you money and keep you away from the problems that can arise when there is no third party involvement. Always keep in mind that a good part of, if not the entire fee, can be earned during skillful negotiations. Many sellers do not realize this and focus only on the dollar amount they pay the broker.

The Power of Third Party Negotiators

Throughout the history of the world the best negotiators have made the impossible possible. They have closed distances between opposing parties and found productive ways to reach fair and meaningful compromises. Labor disputes almost always fall into the hands of third party negotiators. The power of negotiations is at the heart of the real estate business. If I had to choose only three qualities that would be critical to agent selection, they would be: skill at negotiations, marketing enthusiasm, and integrity.

Many thousands of dollars are made or lost at the time of negotiations. Not having a third party to handle this part of the process can put excessive pressure on both buyers and sellers and sometimes emotions can ride the opportunity right over the cliff.

This is all being mentioned because selling real estate is not always as simple as saying, "If we sell it at $400,000 and pay a 5% commission, we end up netting $380,000." In many instances the skills of the negotiator can help bring that sale price up another $15,000. On a commission of 5%, that "extra negotiated amount" only cost $750 in commissions earned but made the seller an extra $14,250 in net dollars. A significant part of the entire commission can be earned back when a third party agent works to prove value resulting in a high offer. Look at the big picture.

The Auction Option

During very strong seller markets a self-initiated auction can help sell a home for even more than the listing price. This happens when a number of buyers want the same property and end up being told to submit their best bid for the house. All the bids are usually reviewed by the broker, the seller, and the seller's attorney, if desirable.

Sellers who find themselves in this position are not only in the drivers seat but they also own the road. Auctions may only be viable during very strong seller markets or in areas where demand outpaces supply, but they are becoming far more common than in the past. They certainly avoid the concern for selling a home for less money that it's worth and they prove once again that the market determines price. Not to take advantage of that auction alternative could prove to actually cost a seller money.

"CHICKEN AND EGG"
REAL ESTATE TRANSACTIONS

We have already discussed why most residential homes sales are completed by real estate companies. Perhaps this sounded a bit like an advertisement to use a real estate company when you sell your home, but that wasn't the intent. Its intent was to make you think clearly about all the possibilities and implications of your decision. The last thing you should do is approach selling your home with a "let's give it a try and see what happens" attitude. This is particularly true if you are leveraging the purchase of a new home with the sale of your present property.

Which Came First: The Purchase or the Sale?

Perhaps this question is a bit easier to answer than the one about the chicken and the egg. In many cases buyers decide they want to find a new residence before putting up their present property for sale. Sometimes all it takes is a call from an agent with a great lead.

In fact, few homeowners sell their homes before knowing where and what they are going to move to. Sometimes they may decide to rent or live with family until other matters are settled, but even in that case, they know where they are going to live.

The answer for many buyers is to find the house they want first and then act quickly to sell their present home. (If the buyer has nothing to sell, of course, it certainly simplifies the transaction.) Keep in mind that selling your home in strong seller's markets can help ease the fear of buying a home first and then having to sell your current residence to pay for it. Always assess the market conditions carefully before signing any purchase agreement. If you currently own a home it is wise to know the value of your property before you start your home search, because the equity in your residence will most likely be transferred to your next house.

In some cases the move from one home to another can present certain problems. Coordinating all the key elements of a move requires great focus. There are financial issues, closing dates, obtaining movers, utility changes, address changes and other important issues that can make this a planning challenge. Even sellers moving only five houses away can run into serious problems. Usually it is the distance in thinking between buyers and sellers that causes problems, not the distance between homes.

Get It Right with a Planned Margin of Safety

Some people count on every dollar from the sale of their home to buy a new one. This is not always wise; a 5% difference between what you expect to get from your sale and what you actually receive can be a significant figure. The "business plan" approach previously discussed for buying a home applies to selling your home as well. Lay out a clear and concise financial plan before you make a decision to move. Be sure you have extra funds set aside in case you need them. The individuals who run the most risk are the ones who need to have everything go exactly as planned. This is not a sound business strategy. Adjust your needs accordingly so that in any scenario you have a comfortable margin of safety.

There are risks when people decide to move from one home to another, but none is greater than getting stuck with two homes, a frightening thought for even the most secure home owners. Careful attention to planning and realistic goals can limit that risk. Keeping emotions in check and executing a business plan is the best way to make a seamless transition from one home to another.

It's Not Necessarily Wise to Retain the Same Agent for Both Transactions

With another house under contract, the pressure is on to get the existing homestead sold. If a real estate agent was involved in the purchase of your new home it is very likely that he or she will want to help you sell your existing house, too. This is especially true if it is a local move. All of this may work out just fine, but do not assume the process is automatic. The agent who found you a house may not be the best choice for listing and marketing your current home. Some agents are very strong on selling, but do not do as well at listing and visa versa. There is a lot at stake here because you have two huge assets being managed at the same time. It would not be uncommon for the combined values of the new purchase and your existing home to exceed $750,000 or more.

There may also be some conflicts of interest if the agent is representing you on both ends, but these can be worked out easily with simple disclosure forms. Most agents will explain these in detail.

What a Seller Needs to Know

The average seller has many things to consider: price, marketing plan, number of open houses, the amount of advertising the broker plans to do, track record of the agent, office and company support, length of time of the listing, closing date, rules and regulations of the MLS. network, lock box operations and safety concerns for who will be coming into their home, information on seller disclosure, buyer inspections, inspection fees, legal fees, contract information, deposits held, what they have to do to prepare the home for showing, the commission to be charged, and how long will it take to sell and close the house. All of these are important and can affect the fine-tuning of your home prior to presenting it on the market.

Competition Can Bring out the Best in the Best and the Worst in the Worst

Every real estate agent is associated with a real estate company. On the buying end, your needs will be quite different from your needs on the selling side. Select your broker very carefully. As previously mentioned, it is best to interview several agents for the job. You want to get as much value as you can from the effort being made by the agent and his or her company. As in most areas of business, it is not what you pay that counts the most—it is the value you receive. Competition to represent your home is going to be keen, and if you are patient in the agent selection process, you will receive exactly what you need in quality service. People react differently to competition. Sometimes it will bring the best out in the best and the worst out in the worst. Be sure not to simply list your home with an agent who is just a personal friend or social acquaintance.

Now that you have found the right home, clear the decks. Do not automatically list your home with the agent who found your new home. Conduct a full broker search for the best agent. It is highly possible that your agent might be the right choice to help with the sale of your home, but you owe it to yourself and your assets to be sure.

Does Size Matter?

Today there are many large real estate companies with a full line of customer services. The biggest ones are really a chain of local offices linked together by a common business culture. They are fully capable of delivering the very best local service. As in all fields being large has its advantages. Still, ask questions about company training programs for agents and brokers. When a company's emphasis has been placed on education and training, the consumer stands to benefit. However, the size of an organization alone does not matter if the agent you select is not talented, knowledgeable, honest and determined to help you in every possible way.

Real estate is a local business regardless of how many offices an organization has on its roster. Sometimes a higher quality agent works in a smaller local office and with access to the same multiple listing service can provide all the services you need to get the job done. In general, the full service organizations have access to greater advertising leverage and a multitude of buyer and seller friendly ancillary services. Not every company is the very best in every town they operate in. Strong, local "niche" brokers can still deliver the services you need, but a high quality agent backed by a full service organization is tough to beat.

Real Estate Companies Always Want Listings

Real estate companies love to obtain listings. It helps them to increase their market share. Because of that, they will make every effort to please you. An office visit to several companies will be one of the best real estate moves you can make. It places you in control of the situation. The manager will cooperate fully in helping you to conduct a search for the agent most suited to your needs.

After obtaining managers' recommendations from at least two different companies, plan to set up appointments with each of the hand-picked agents at your home. The sales associates will also want to do that in order to view your house and learn first-hand about your home's selling strengths and weaknesses. Keep in mind that almost every home has both. Like the tennis player we talked about awhile back, the way to improve your game is to strengthen your weakest areas. If you choose not to do this, those weaknesses will take away from the home's strengths and result in fewer dollars from the buyer.

TIME FOR THE HOUSE DOCTOR TO
11 MAKE A HOUSE CALL

Sometimes an agent will bring other members of his or her office to see your home. This usually takes place prior to meeting with you for the actual listing presentation. This group of realtors will inspect your house and make an appointment to present their findings later that day or the next day. This is a great service for all, because you will have a variety of opinions from different agents and you will soon get the facts as to current market conditions in a competitive market analysis. In some parts of the country agents measure every room as part of their house inspection. In other markets total square footage is a key factor. (Generally speaking, total square footage is always used in marketing new construction.)

Look for the attention potential agents pay to the details of your home. Do they go into each room, check all the closets, visit the basement and attic areas? Do they walk the entire property? If they are not going to be thorough on the inspection of your home, with the potential for a listing at stake, then they just might not be the right one to market your property. The agent handling your home should know every possible detail almost as well as you do. He or she should have lots of questions for the home owner. For your part, provide any information you have about your property and be sure to include any special features of the house. Do not assume all will be covered. It is not a question of who is right or wrong; it is just more important that all the amenities are covered properly. This is one "house call" you want to participate in strongly.

The Day of Reckoning

Before you signed a contract on your new home, you should have received information on the value of your present one. If several months have passed, it may be necessary to revisit market conditions again. Listen carefully to what the agents have to say, being careful to not react until their entire presentation is over and done. Never tell an agent what you think your house is worth until you hear what the realtor has to say first. Never tell them what you have to "get" for the place. Some agents will try hard to hear the price you want in order to slant their opinion more favorably to yours, but this is the last thing you want to have happen. It would be like going to a doctor for a diagnosis of a health problem, only to find that the doctor's main objective was to tell you what you want to hear.

Choosing what appears to be the path of least resistance will probably present more problems for you than accepting the candid appraisal of an experienced realtor. A true professional will be honest and forthright about market conditions. An inflated market appraisal will only hurt the seller in the long run. Buyers could care less about what you have to "get" for your home. In most situations, if they sense urgency on the seller's part, they will look to take advantage of that in any forthcoming negotiations.

Go to School on the Listing Presentations

When the agent comes to your house to make the listing presentation, you have an excellent opportunity to judge his or her integrity and overall knowledge and marketing skills. Consider this to be a job interview, because that's what it is. There will be many questions and perhaps even an awkward moment or two. How the agent handles all of these situations is a wonderful opportunity for the owner to experience an agent's skills in action. If the agent does not impress you, then how is he going to spread the word about your house with the necessary enthusiasm? How is he going to represent you when the negotiations get intense? Does he have problem solving skills? Look for genuine and sincere interest in the marketing of your home. When all the sales talents and marketing tools are there and the enthusiasm is high, you will know why searching for the right company and agent is the single most important step you can take in selling your home.

High on the list of talents a good agent must have are: strong negotiating skills, marketing expertise, enthusiasm, a keen sense of timing, a through understanding of urgency, local knowledge and people skills. These attributes alone can more than justify the participation of a professional.

The Competitive Market Analysis Competes

In addition to information about their particular office, advertising, open houses, market conditions, and their company, most agents end up basing a listing presentation on the "Competitive Market Analysis" or "CMA" That is the document used to appraise your home and establish the suggested price. Most CMAs include the following information: recent comparable homes that have closed title, homes that are under contract where the selling price is known and the closing is pending, and homes currently on the market that will be competing directly with your home. Agents will show you pictures and descriptions of these examples. Spend time reviewing this information; don't just go through the motions. Ask questions about the homes and look to see if the comparables make sense to you as the seller. Keep in mind that although homes are not like snowflakes (no two alike) there are major personality differences even in the same type of home. Land parcels vary, locations differ, and the quality of amenities varies from home to home. Making a direct eye-to-eye comparison is not that easy to do. Oftentimes the value of the property size is overlooked when sellers compare homes. Land values alone can make dwelling comparisons more difficult to understand. Sometimes one house is better than another, similar home, but the main difference lies in the land size and value of the location.

Why You Should Ignore National Averages

When you hear information on national averages for home sale appreciation, do not apply them to your specific market. Remember, they are "averages." For example, if a recent real estate report stated that the national averages for appreciation were between 6% and 8% annually, you would not want to apply those figures to your specific home. If you lived in a town in the Northeast the appreciation on homes could have run closer to 12% per year for the same time period. Regional and national figures rarely seem to make sense for any one locality, although they do work well to show overall trends in the marketplace.

THE ARROW LEAVES THE BOW:
SETTING A PRICE

The listing presentation will eventually lead to that moment you have been anticipating, determining what the price will be for your home when it goes on the market. Obviously, a higher suggested price than expected from an agent is always good news, but price is only one factor. Although you may judge the suggested price against your own expectations, it does not mean that your expectations were necessarily correct.

When there's a difference of opinion, some sellers become defensive. They may even actually start to "haggle" with their own agent, citing neighborhood sales patterns to prove their house is worth more than the agent suggested. Seller's pride may surface as the seller explains how much better his or her home is than the one that sold across the street. However, better carpet and more expensive appliances will not make up for a poorer location or smaller lot size. As noted several times, the closed files of the agent should work to clarify any discrepancies in neighborhood real estate values. I would question the quality of the agent who does not have that kind of information available. Facts have a way of clearing the air. Keep in mind that this is an opportunity to gain insight into the agent's ability to explain clearly the reasons he or she has for suggesting the proper price or price range. A polite but firm agent is a sign of someone who will in all likelihood be a good negotiator for you.

Get a Second Opinion

Sometimes owners feel very positive about an agent and the listing price and decide to go with the first agent with whom they meet. But it is wiser to be patient and seek another point of view. I do not think you would want a major medical operation with out a second opinion. Selling a house is also a major operation, a major business operation.

You will always learn something from an additional presentation. Most of us would not think twice about getting several estimates when we are ready to have our house painted or vinyl-sided. Either of these expenses only represents a very small percentage of the value of the home; why wouldn't you get a second opinion when you're dealing with the TOTAL value?

When the next agent arrives, you already have more information than when the first one showed up. You will know more about market conditions, price information, terms, commissions, and most of the other information necessary to get your home ready to market. So, you're a few steps higher on the seller ladder. The view will already be different from that vantage point.

Keep in mind that your goal is to find the best agent to sell your home, not the one that tells all you want to hear. Again, hold silent as to any feelings you have about price. Never talk about other home sales in your town or on your own street. They tend to give a close estimate of what you may be thinking in regard to your own home's value. Let the agent do his or her presentation. Learn about the company, marketing plans, seller support systems, MLS guidelines, and suggestions to improve your home before marketing.

Seller Beware

When you have several brokers in to preview your home and present their suggested prices, you may find that they differ significantly. How can that happen? Real estate is not a science, and even when you mix the same ingredients in the same way at the same time, the results may come out differently. Appraisal of homes can be very personal and, as stated before, there is a lot of emotion in the market place. Homes have personalities just like people. In some cases comparables are not that easy to find during certain times in the market place. Remember that sales that occurred more than six months ago may or may not have significant value for the CMA.

Keep in mind that there is no one set price for anything, not just real estate properties. Prices vary because of supply and demand. Shelf position can change daily. If five properties came on the market in the same price range as yours, the "shelf position" of your home would be affected. If three properties that were in competition with your home all sold, your shelf position could change immediately. Therefore it is highly recommended that you have a weekly evaluation with your agent until your house is sold.

Agent Presentations Are Not Offers to Purchase

One of the biggest mistakes a seller can make is to list his or her home with the agent or company that promises them the highest listing price. Think about that for a minute. There are some agents who only want to find out what you want for the house or, even worse, what you have to get to buy another property. They know that if they meet your price expectations they might increase their chances of getting the listing. That is the kind of agent you do not want to work with under any circumstances. If they want to "buy the listing" let them write a check for the full price they suggest and meet you at the closing table.

This is a very common trap to fall into as a homeowner. As a seller you are anticipating that your home will fly off the market. You have brokers coming to your home wanting to list your property. You can feel like a rock star at a concert. Promises will be moving around like swarming bees. Now if office Z tells you it thinks you can get $380,000 for your home while office X tells you should get $340,000, who in their right mind would not take the higher figure? That is a $40,000 difference. Now let's push the "return to reality" button. The prices suggested by the two agents ARE NOT OFFERS TO PURCHASE YOUR HOME. They are value opinions based on their interpretation of the market information and current conditions. Do not treat them as offers to purchase, when at best, they are only estimates of value.

Get Inside the Buyer's Head

Buyers tend to stay within certain price ranges when they are looking to purchase. For example, if a buyer was qualified to buy a home up to $375,000 she could easily look at homes up to or even over that figure, especially if she knew she had additional funds to use for a down payment. If a home came on the market for $405,000, she just might not look at it if $400,000 was her cut-off price. This is especially true for first time buyers who tend to have less flexibility when purchasing. Most buyers have a "mental" price line they do not want to cross.

However, if that same home was placed on the market at $399,000, that buyer just might take a look. Now if she loves the house and found the value to be the best she had seen, she just might tap those extra dollars for the purchase. The lesson here is to increase buyer activity on your home by keeping away from price "barriers." Sometimes a difference of only $100 can widen the buyer pool. A home listed at $499,900 instead of $500,000 has strength in the $450,000- $499,999 range. Once it crosses the $500,000 threshold, it now has to compete with a variety of homes over $500,000, namely homes up to $550,000 or even more.

"Bookends" Can Help Set the Price Range

The best way to determine price range is to establish "bookends" of value. The "bookend" on the left would represent a low figure that would most likely make a house fly off the market. The one on the right would establish a high price where the house would simply sit and go nowhere. The bookends are therefore the extremes of the price range. Sometimes it is easier to determine the lows and the highs than the so-called "exact price;" it's certainly easier to find the sensible middle ground this way.

For example, if a price of $425,000 was the low end of

your range, one that would be a no-brainer for any potential buyer, the house would leave the market at the speed of Mach 1. Now let's say $500,000 is the price that would take the home out of the competition, labeled "overpriced" by nearly everyone. Bookend $425,000 and bookend $500,000 have given you a broad range to work with. Split that difference and we have $37,500, so let's add that amount to the "Mach 1" price, bringing you to $462,500. This is a good mid-range price, but you could probably go a little higher, like $479,900. (Notice that we've just avoided the much higher-sounding $480,000!)

In any case, you always want to stay away from the "bookends." Neither will produce a satisfactory outcome.

Proceed with Caution

If you based your decision for broker selection only on price, all a second broker would have to do is keep raising their price estimate until they got the listing. This fantasy price war might continue, but the logical elements necessary to market your home would be lost in the process. Be realistic when you consider all the terms and conditions involved in the selling process. Emotion wants to run the show but sensibility, logic, knowledge and a business plan will get you to where you want to be in much better shape. Stay focused on selecting the best agent and company to represent you. If all you got out of the listing presentations were suggested prices, you may have lost track of your real goals.

Select Your Agent and Form a Team

When the listing presentations are over you will be ready to make your decision on the agent and the company to represent you. Look for an agent who loves your home and has been successful in your local area with recent home sales. Be sure they are working full time in every way. Evaluate their negotiating skills by asking for examples of how they work with buyers and other brokers. Be sure the CMA was honest and portrayed a true picture of the market conditions.

Look for strong problem solving skills in an agent. Ask yourself this question: would I buy a home from this person? If the answer is no, move on. Remember that enthusiasm is a great mover and shaker. The agents that possess a strong sense of urgency can keep everything moving in the right direction.

With the decision made you will be asked to execute a listing agreement, and the agent will explain the other documents pertinent to the listing and MLS regulations. You will be encouraged to place a lock box on your home for easy access. These are very secure and helpful to agents and buyers, especially when no one is home for a showing. In some areas the MLS keeps accurate accounting of who enters your home via a lock box. It is a good security measure for homeowners. Remember, the easier it is to have access to your home, the more showings that can occur.

If for some reason this is not the way you want to go, the agent will work out other means of access with a key in their office. In some cases the listing broker accompanies all showings by other agents.

PREPARING YOUR HOME
FOR VIEWING

Most sellers want to know what they have to do to make their homes create the most positive first impression. If your realtor has not provided you with a "punch list" of items to prepare your home, be sure to request it. Put aside your pride and ask for the most honest input possible. Your strength will be your ability to recognize and correct any weak areas. If your house requires paint and repairs, get them done before the first buyer ever steps foot in the doorway. Even if you're short on time, doing what has to be done to make your home "ready for the dance" will pay off big-time. You don't want to be in the position of having to tell a potential buyer that "if you just did this and this and this" the house might look better. All that does is further highlight the weak features of the home.

Make a list of all the projects and check them off as you complete each item. Have the broker back to the house to check your progress. Some hard work and usually a small investment in paint and hardware can usually give you a decent return. Your home just might look so good that you decide not to sell it!

Long Term Care Is Best

There is a lot to be said for homeowners who take excellent care of their homes from the day they leave the closing table. Long-term house care is the best care of all. Discriminating buyers can usually tell the difference between a house that has had continuous top-notch maintenance and those that were cleaned up over a weekend.

It's a lot like selling a car. Some people do not even take the time to vacuum out the inside or wash and wax a car before showing it to a buyer. Telling a buyer that all he or she has to do is apply a good coat of wax for it to be a "beauty" is hardly reassuring. It will only raise doubts in the buyer's mind. On the other hand, when you go to purchase an automobile that has complete service records and is in excellent condition you are more willing to pay the asking price or close to it. In regard to care and preparation, homes can be viewed very much the same in most cases. Your house is a significant part of your total estate. Keep it in the best condition possible every year so when the time comes to sell, your "punch list" of things to do will fit on the inside of a match cover.

Turn On the Agents and They Turn On the Customers

Just as your home goes on the market, your listing agent will probably arrange to bring a group of realtors in for a home preview. In most cases you will be given advance notice so you can be out of the house that day, allowing the realtors to speak with candor about your home. Hanging around during a home preview just might keep the agents from expressing their true opinions about the place. Honest feedback is the only kind you want to hear. When you go over the comments listen carefully and do not take any remarks personally. This is a business deal. Try to concentrate on the financial and marketing aspects of the transaction. Before you respond to feedback, ask yourself this question, "Am I reacting like a home owner or a home seller?" Your role is that of the seller.

Like a hot stock tip, news spreads quickly about new listings. Upon leaving a house many sales representatives will call their clients immediately and attempt to set up an appointment to show the house. They also will tell other brokers in their offices about your home. Because not all local realtors will be able to see your home at the preview, word of mouth throughout the real estate grapevine will be the next best thing. Having a listing agent who spreads the word daily is a great asset to any seller.

ON THE MARKET!

The big day has arrived. Your home is on the market and you've done everything asked of you to get it ready. A sign is up on the front lawn. A listing is on the internet and in the offices of the MLS members. Now the world knows your home is for sale.

Naturally, you wish the home would sell to the very first buyer who sees it so you could put all of this to rest and resume your normal life style. It is not uncommon for this to happen and when it does, seller's remorse can come on like a bad cold: "I sold it too cheap." Generally speaking, however, during normal market conditions the first offer you get in writing may turn out to be the best offer.

What to Look For and What to Look At

Once your home is on the market, the number one thing to look for is customer activity. You can monitor this in a variety of different ways: the number of inquiries from other agents directed at the listing agent; the quality of the inquiries; feedback from the agents who previewed your home; and number of showings. A good listing agent will call every broker who shows your house and ask for honest feedback. I would even suggest that you require your listing agent to keep a written log of showings and comments of both buyers and their realtors.

During your home's first two weeks on the market there should be a flurry of activity with a lot of showings. Activity is your "barometer" for your home's marketability. A lot of great activity and no written offers might tell you that your house is overpriced for the market. A low level of activity might tell you the same thing.

"Shelf Position" Changes Constantly in the Real Estate "Store"

Picture your house sitting on a shelf in the "store" alongside all the other homes in the same general price range. When your listing goes on the market your home will take a position on that shelf. As shelf position changes when new properties come on the market and others are taken off, especially those that are in your general price range, you'll want your home to continue to stand out and not just sit there. In food stores items are rotated according to expiration dates. On the real estate shelf you want to be sure your home does not expire, either.

Your sales representative should continuously update you as to your market position. During times of inventory shortages, the sellers benefit the most. Short supply provides fewer comparisons and that can cause buyers to move quickly in securing the houses they want. The fewer homes on the shelf, the better it is for the seller. Not so good for the buyer.

During the first two weeks of that first month on the market, you should have an ample number of showings and some "return lookers." Sometimes first showings just happen because your home is new on the market, but when a buyer comes back to the house the second time, it is a very positive sign. Your chances of receiving an offer have now increased. The fact that buyers return for a second viewing is also an indication that your home is probably in the correct price range.

30 Days Hath September, and So Does Your Prime Selling Window

Experience strongly suggests that the first 30-45 days on the market can be the most critical for home sellers. During this time period the ultimate judge of your home's value will be serious and qualified buyers looking to purchase a home. During this initial period of time, certain events should occur in order to prove your home is in the right price range, though nothing proves it better than a sale and a closing of title.

Keep in mind that from the first day you place your home on the market all opinions, estimates of value, and information regarding your home are going to be tested. The marketplace tells the truth because it is where "the rubber hits the road." Either your home will gain traction with positive activity or it will be ready for a tire change. The real estate road show has begun. If you have not received any written offers at the end of the first 30 days, be prepared to make a thorough and complete evaluation of the activity (or lack of it) so far. If your house is still getting a lot of interest, you can probably hold off on making any changes for several more weeks.

Specifically, look for answers to the following questions: How many showings took place? How many buyers returned for a second look? How many written offers were there? What were the comments from the potential buyers who viewed your home?

Did those buyers go on and purchase other homes? If so, what did the other homes have that triggered a sale? What did the other brokers think of your home's position in the market place? Use this information to re-evaluate your marketing strategy. Examine all marketing efforts, including the individual efforts of your listing sales representative. Your agent should be acting as a sort-of general contractor, coordinating all effort in a positive drive towards a closing.

If it is obvious that the activity on your home has slowed down and the number of showings is decreasing, then the time for change is upon you. At first it is quite common to make excuses (like saying bad weather kept people away), which is only natural as you try to stick to the original marketing position. Just about everyone does this to a point, but the fact is rationalizations and excuses do not sell homes.

Overpricing Is Like a Red Light That Never Changes

Let's cut to the chase here: nothing hurts your home more than overpricing. How can the very best homes sit on the market and not sell when so called "dogs" are sold in a few weeks? How can a house in excellent condition, on a quiet street in one of the best towns in the area, still be on the market after three months? How can a listing that was advertised 25 times still be on the market? How can a property that had 8 open houses still be on the market? How can a house that was shown 50 times not be sold? How can a home that had written offers still be on the market? Overpricing.

This is something that sellers tend to go into denial over, using excuses like "bad weather" to explain the lack of interest. (If this were the case, homes would only sell on sunny days.) Sometimes a listing agent will present all the right feedback but the seller will still refuse to make a change. But buyers always determine the ultimate value of a home. When enough of them have seen a home and not one written offer has come in, turn the page, and turn it quickly. Remember that even a low offer in writing is proof that someone was willing to sign his name with the intent of buying your home. When there have been no offers, it is a warning light for the seller to make a change. Even more alarming is a precipitous decrease in showings.

Being in the wrong price range is a lot like being out of hearing range: potential buyers are just not getting your message! Today's buyers are smart and they do not want to waste their time looking at homes that are not competitively priced. The faster you get to the right target range, the more the house will sell for. Bread tends to get stale in about a week. Homes can start after 30 days.

Overexposure at the Wrong Price Can Hurt

The sellers who can get hurt the most are the ones who simply do not respond to the lack of activity on their homes. And a small adjustment of, say, $10,000, can be worse than no price decrease at all (unless it changes the range, i.e. $505,000 to $495,000). When a property sits for a long period of time with no activity and no major adjustments by the seller, it starts to fade from the minds of salespeople as well. This is a natural reaction and it almost always ends up with sellers getting far less for their houses than if they had acted right away. No one wants stale bread. If a potential buyer asks how long a home been on the market and the answer is 120 days, they're probably thinking something's wrong with it. Buyer doubt is something you do not want to raise. It has a way of costing the seller far more than it should.

It is critical that sellers approach the idea of reducing the list price of their homes with an open and receptive attitude. To repeat, the only ones who are going to establish the ultimate value of your home are buyers with offers in hand.

It's a Lot Like Fishing

Have you ever fished for a few hours, without getting so much as a strike? That's a lot like having your house on the market for 45 days without getting even a nibble. In both cases you're probably using the wrong "lure." Just as some people can fish the same stream with good success, the fact that you are coming up empty means that you should probably re-examine the kind of bait you're using. That bait could be a meaningful reduction in the price "lure" of your home.

Each "Link" Moves You Closer to Your Goal

If your home has finally "found" its value and activity has picked up, showings will lead to second showings, which will eventually lead to written offers. Offers lead to negotiations. Negotiations lead to final agreements. Agreements lead to executed contracts. Contracts lead to contingencies. Satisfied contingencies lead to closings of title. Closing of titles lead to celebrations! Each of these is a very important "link" on the chain that will help connect you from one residence to another.

Only the Seller Has the Key to the Truth "Vault"

Oftentimes the reasons given for lack of activity on a home are so sugar-coated with rationalizations and excuses that it's as if the truth were locked up in a vault. Sellers hold the key to the "vault." Most friends and even some agents will just keep telling the seller what he wants to hear, not what he has to hear. An agent may be telling his client what he wants to hear just to avoid conflict, but in the end he is doing the seller a disservice. Professional realtors ought to be able to "sell the truth;" the top producers know how to do this. Although providing excuses and rationalizations can provide temporary relief, they never sell houses.

CONSIDERING
AN OFFER

An Offer Is Not an Offer If It's Not in Writing

Sellers and agents must be careful not to entertain any verbal offers or other attempts to "feel out" what sort of price a seller will consider. Written offers are the only real offers. Talk is cheap, and sometimes it even has negative implications. If buyers are not serious enough to write a check as a deposit and sign an offer-to-purchase agreement, then they are not "in the game." They are in the stands, watching the game and playing Monday morning quarterback. If a verbal offer is brought to you or your agent, it's best not to respond at all. Give all the information about the property you want, but give no verbal signal as to what would be an acceptable price. Suggest to potential buyers that in the best interests of all parties they should put their thoughts in writing. When that has been done with an offer-to-purchase agreement, along with a check, you will be more than happy to respond in writing as well.

There Is More to an Offer Than the Price

Once your home is on the market and the momentum for a sale starts to build, the seller must be alert to the full meaning of each and every offer. Initially, most of us are interested in the price first. However, the price alone does not mean you have a great offer. For example, if you had your home on the market for $295,000 and you got an offer of $290,000, you would in all likelihood be pleased with that. However, further examination might show that the buyer was only putting 5% down on the property, meaning that the buyer would have to qualify for a 95% mortgage. Yes, there may be a pre-approval letter from a bank, but in a changing marketplace there may be a problem with the loan-to-value ratio of the home. If the appraisal comes in lower on the home, the qualifications may change. The strength of the buyer comes into play with all the other factors. Most sellers would prefer a stronger down payment, such as an offer of $285,000 with 25% down.

The closing date is critical as well. A deferred closing date can mean time lost, and time lost has a price, too. Most sellers have a specific time period in mind to close title. If you had an offer that was satisfactory in price but the closing date was off by several months, you would have to calculate the cost and risk of keeping the home longer than you intended. An offer for a higher amount but a longer than desired closing date might not be as good as a lower offer and the desire to close as soon as possible. Always factor in the emotional stress associated with waiting longer than you planned to close title. When it comes to seeking a closing, I always suggest the sooner the better.

Contingencies Are Exactly That

Most contracts contain contingencies. These are legal requirements by the seller and buyer that must be completed within a specific time period. The agreements of the contract are dependent on the satisfactory completion of contractual contingencies in a timely manner.

Legal issues are important. These may vary from state to state, but most real estate agents use realtor-approved contracts that establish a period of time for attorney review of the documents. During that time period neither party is bound to the contract terms and conditions until their own attorney approves the contract or makes changes in agreement with the other party's attorney. This sometimes takes a few days to work out, but it is intended to protect both parties from potentially serious problems. Generally speaking the period of time for the attorney review is three business days. (If the attorneys draw up the contracts themselves, then this three-day waiting period may not apply.) In addition to the mortgage-qualification contingency, the contract might include inspections of the following: a home's structural integrity, oil tank, termites, insects, rodents, carpenter ants, septic systems, water testing and environmental issues such as radon, lead paint, and urea-formaldehyde. In some states there may be other items particular to a region or locality. Each contingency will have a specific time period assigned to it and a legal clause stating the rights of the seller and the buyer.

An offer may also include specific items included in the purchase, such as drapes, kitchen appliances, and sometimes even furniture.

Make It a Counteroffer, Not a Counter Punch

Assuming that most offers are acceptable in some aspects but not fully acceptable in others, you will want to make a counteroffer to the buyer. Respond to the entire offer, not just the price. That is the right thing to do in every case. Accepted areas of an offer should be acknowledged, along with a counter proposal for the areas not in accordance with the seller's desires. Most people just respond to the price and that can cause an isolated price war.

Take the "punch" out of your counteroffer. To begin with, always thank the buyer for presenting a written offer on your home. That's a great way to get things on a positive footing, regardless of the offer. It will warm the buyer to you as the seller and encourage honest and forthright negotiations. The closing date, the contingencies for the inspections, items that are included in the sale, the mortgage contingency, or any other item that is acceptable should receive a positive response from you.

Perhaps the price is the only item that is not acceptable. There is no exact price for a home, so do not get hung up in trying to find one. If a buyer thinks he can get a better value elsewhere, he should satisfy that curiosity before responding again.

Negotiations can only work to everyone's advantage if all heads stay cool. Keep in mind that you are selling a huge asset, but you are not selling your family. They only get the house, not your first-born child, although at times it may feel like this is what is happening. Emotions can make negotiations break down very quickly. Stay focused on the business issues. Try not to split hairs; pick your battles wisely. Usually when disputes come up over small items they work against the bigger, more important issues. Concentrate on what counts the most and the smaller issues will settle themselves.

Waiting for a "Sale" to Make Your Sale

You might get a great offer, but one that is contingent on the buyer selling his home. In some areas of the country this is not even considered to be bona fide offer. When the purchase of your home is dependent on a buyer selling his home first, you should keep your house on the market. Make no binding legal agreements with this kind of buyer. If they truly want your home they will do what they have to do to get their home sold, or plan to buy your home without a contingency for the sale of their home. Contingency sales are not sales, they are agreements in "hoping" and they can lack full commitment. Opinions on this sort of contingency can vary from state to state, so be sure to check local practices carefully.

Close, But Not Close Enough

Treat any offer that has strong terms and conditions with care. Keep in mind that it is the strength of the buyer that will take you to the closing table, not the price. When the price can be agreed upon with a strong buyer, then you will have an excellent chance of changing the name on the title to your home.

Negotiations can break down for a variety of reasons. Apprehension on the part of the buyer continues to grow if the offer is not accepted within a reasonable time period. The buyer has more and more time to talk with friends, fellow workers, family members and all the other real estate "experts" wandering the hills. Usually the more opinions you ask for, the more confused you will become. When too much time passes there is a tendency for the intensity of the deal to fade away. That is why it is so important to strike while the iron is hot. When that iron is hot, it should signal that time is of the essence. Momentum is an invisible force that can make or break a real estate transaction. When it is lost, it is not so easy to regain.

If a sale fails to happen, try to regain your momentum. Regardless of the outcome, learn from what happened and get right back up on the horse that threw you. The longer you wait, the harder it will be to recover. The agent should get that buyer out immediately to see other homes. The seller should stay strong in attitude and make changes only if they make good sense. The buyer has to keep on with his or her search and believe that the right home is still out there.

Connect All the Dots

Very few things in life are ever perfect. When you buy or sell your home it is important to look for fairness on all sides. When the right elements line up, tie down the terms and conditions in a most expeditious manner. Enlist the help of your attorney, agent, inspectors, or whoever else is needed to blaze the trail to the closing.

Stay focused on each and every part of the process. If you find something is not going according to the contract, act on it immediately. Always approach all problems with concern and enough patience to consider all points of view. Remember that having to go all the way back to "go" can cost you in time and money. Transactions have fallen through over such illogical things as fear, ego battles, and lack of communication. Maintain a strong desire to find solutions, not create problems.

Compromise is the word of the day. Once again, a third party negotiator can help keep the necessary balance between the parties.

16 FROM THE TRUNK IN THE ATTIC: MISCELLANEOUS TIPS AND ADVICE

Amber Light Transition Markets

One of the most frequently asked questions in real estate has to do with the overall market condition. Is it a buyer's market or a seller's market? Most of the time it will be one or the other. However, I have found that knowing when the market is changing its direction is also worth recognizing. Let's call that market a "transition market." When is the trend moving from a buyer's market to a seller's market or vice-versa? Not an easy question to answer in regard to any kind of major market.

Very few people can predict the top or the bottom of the stock market. Millions try each year, and millions miss. Not many people can predict the top or the bottom of the real estate market, either. Millions try, millions miss. Hitting a moving target is not so easy to do. And in this case the more complex the target, the more difficult the task.

In past markets some buyers were hurt when they purchased at the very top of the market and then had to sell within a few years. During very strong markets it is easy to forget the down times, but they happened and can happen again. How do you spot a transition market? This is the market that is created as the market begins to move away from its current position. It is the flashing light period, the amber light warning that there is going to be a change.

When you are in a sellers market for a long time, everyone will know it, the barber, the mailman, even the birds in the trees. Everyone will think it will never end. But that in itself may be a sign that the top has been reached already. When everyone thinks it is going to keep going up and up and last forever, forever has a way of turning the page. The same holds true of a buyer's market. We all know that nothing stays the same. Change is inevitable, but how we react to it doesn't have to be.

In the summer of 1988 a local newspaper ran the headline, "Waiting for the End of the Glut." It talked about the "bear" market in northern New Jersey. The article went on to show how the number of homes on the market had swelled from around 1,700 in 1986 to over 3,700 in 1988. The average number of days on the market before a sale took place went from 54 days in 1986 to 71 days in 1987 and to 118 days in 1988. There were stories of sellers offering free cars and trips to the Caribbean to potential buyers. The people who got hurt the most during this "bear" home market were the ones who purchased a home at the top of that market and then had to turn around and sell it as the market went down. Those that waited it out saw the market turn around again and head back north. That low in 1988 lasted for quite a few years, but it was eventually replaced by a strong and growing seller's market.

Trading Spaces

When homeowners decide to sell their homes and then purchase another in the same market at the same time, they are usually on safe ground in regard to value exchange.

If several years later they look back and see the home they sold had moved up significantly in price, they have the comfort of knowing that the home they purchased did the same. In fact, if a buyer moved up in price range on his purchase, then in all likelihood he made even more money on the new purchase than if he had held on to his previous home. The reason is simple. If we assume that the appreciation on homes was 4% for both properties, then 4% of the more expensive home yields more dollars than the previous residence. However, always keep in mind that not all price ranges react at the same time to the same conditions due to supply and demand.

Seller's Markets Establish Seller Control

Let's look at a typical seller's market. Home prices have been going up because demand has outstripped supply. Length of time on the market keeps getting shorter and inventory is at a low level because more homes go off the market than are coming on the market. The real estate store has lots of shelves but most of them are pretty empty. Low interest rates draw buyers into the marketplace and therefore continue to limit home supply. Sellers take a strong position about holding to their prices. They offer to do far less in the area of improvements and other requests of buyers. The sellers are in the driver's seat and they know it. Buyers have to be fast on the "pen draw" to get a house when they have true interest. Auctions on homes start to become commonplace because more than one buyer ends up bidding on the same home. All of these are signs of the times—the seller's times.

It Takes 20/20 Vision

Early warning signs for a market in transition may be hard to spot, but they are out there. If you are in a strong seller's market, look for an increase in the number of homes coming on the market compared to the exit count. Look for the number of days it takes for a home to sell to start to increase. Look for interest rate increases to price some buyers out of the market. Check for price reductions, a signal that homes are taking longer to sell. Most reductions do not occur during the first 30 -45 days, but as fewer homes sell during this time period more homes are being set up for price cutting. In addition, the real estate shelves are starting to fill up with new listings making it all the more important for a home to stand out on the shelf. The transition happens slowly, sort of like when the days start getting shorter as we head toward the winter solstice. Day by day you do not notice it until one day you realize its dark at 6:00 PM. Everyone likes to hang on longer than they should to a good thing, so be careful if the amber light is flashing a change in direction.

A Buyer's Market Has Its Signals, Too

In a buyer's market inventory not only builds as more homes come on the market, but also because homes take longer to sell. As more homes come on the market supply starts to out run demand, prompting sellers to adjust prices accordingly. The shelves in the real estate store are filling up.

Prices may soften at first, then may even adjust downward from the highs of a prolonged seller's market. Prices for new listings entering the market begin to be more realistic.

Buyers start to make more demands of the seller. They may ask sellers to hold a first or second mortgage or include more items (like appliances or drapes) in the sale. Knowing they are at an advantage, buyers may request the seller to make more repairs after the home inspection. They are also more likely to pull out of a deal at the first sign of trouble. Now the same momentum that worked so well for the seller is just as strong for the buyer. In reality, for every inch gained by the seller, it is something taken away from the buyer, and vice-versa. What we do know is that nothing stays the same. The gamble is only on the timing.

To Inspect or Not to Inspect?

Once a written contract has been signed by all parties, the contingencies contained within it are important and critical to both the buyer and the seller. Contingencies for home inspections are standard for most buyers. The importance of this step should not be overlooked. It is strongly advised that a buyer spend ample time searching out the best kind of home inspector possible. The talent in this pool can range from a state certified home inspector, to a retired builder, to a local handy man with a few basic skills. But don't be cheap and have your father-in-law do it just because he happens to know something about plumbing and electricity. Seek names from your attorney or broker and specify that you want the most qualified person available. You want maximum value from this inspection, so look for someone who comes highly recommended and who is perhaps even certified.

Most home inspectors will limit their liability with disclosure statements covering only what they could see on the day of inspection. If you read the fine print you may feel you do not have much recourse if they miss something that costs you later on. As a buyer, I would be on the premises when the inspection is being done. As the homeowner I would also want to be present to answer questions and participate in the entire process.

Look for an inspector who has both structural and practical building experience and will not be afraid to get down and dirty on the inspection day. The roof, attic, basements, foundation and other critical areas need more than a glance and a checked box on a list. In a case of uncertainty most inspectors will err on the side of caution, sometimes causing more concern than is necessary.

The most important elements of a home to check out thoroughly are the roof, foundation, basement, water seepage or entry water into the basement of any kind, sump pump, water softeners, water pressure, water potability testing, toilets, tiles and grouting, structural integrity of the building, all inside and outside masonry work, electrical, plumbing, water pipes, electrical box service amps, hot water heater, heating system, paint, gutters and leaders, drainage, storms windows and screens, patios, brick areas, termites, carpenter ants, post powder beetles, underground oil tanks, urea formaldehyde, lead paint, radon, chimney masonry, fireplace dampers, outside fireplace "caps," air conditioning units, central air conditioning, driveway, cement aprons, garage door openers, door entrances, outside lighting, and general landscaping. In-ground pools require separate inspections by certified pool companies. Other structures on the property, if any, should also be included in the home inspection process. Be sure to determine if the home is in a flood zone, close to any high voltage towers, cell phone towers, or any other potential safety hazard as well.

Always keep in mind that very few homes are going to be perfect; even brand new homes can have problems. Many new homes come with a warranty provided by the builder; in some cases, it is required by the state the home is in. Some companies will sell home warranties for appliances and other major operating systems in the house. I advise careful examination of the benefits, risks and costs associated with these programs before agreeing to them. With regard to new construction, the best home "warranty" is to buy a house from a top quality builder with a solid reputation. With any new home purchase, take the time to talk to other owners who have lived in homes by the same builder. Talking to past customers will serve as a valuable incentive to builder quality and follow-up services. If a problem occurs, where will your builder be and how will he respond? With the proper seller disclosure form, a new home warranty, and a quality home inspection, most buyers should have it all covered.

It's also important to remember the big picture. Don't let small problems that represent a very small part of a home's value steer you away from finalizing the sale. Home inspections usually occur within the first 14 days of the contract and buyer apprehensions may not be completely settled. Sometimes a home inspection works as the wrong reason to get out of a deal. Certainly, if there are serious problems and the seller will not correct them to the buyer's satisfaction, then walking away may be the best thing to do. However, be sure to approach the inspection as an opportunity to find out both the strengths and weakness of the home. Expect both. In most cases the items can be corrected or even overlooked if the other terms and conditions of the contract are satisfactory. During seller's markets, the homeowner will not want to do much in the way of repairs. In a buyer's market they may be willing to do a lot more. Supply and demand can affect all aspects of a transaction.

New insurance issues that complicate the home inspection process have developed in recent years. Many carriers, for example, will not insure a home with an underground oil tank more than ten years old, or they will exclude the liabilities associated with that risk from their coverage. Always check with your local realtor about specific items you should include in your list of contingencies with regard to home inspections and insurance. These, of course, will vary by state and region, but the trend appears to be that insurance carriers are not simply covering any house that comes along. Carrier selectivity is growing and it may not be long before the ability to secure a homeowners policy becomes a contingency itself. (Most mortgage institutions already have this as a requirement before they will lend.)

Be reasonable and fair in your handling of items of concern. Keep your focus on the big picture and the opportunity at hand. Your realtor and/or attorney is in the best position to negotiate and settle any issues related to home inspections. Use their third-party negotiating skills to help smooth the way to a fair and equitable resolution of each situation.

It is best to always expect some things to be in need of repair. I have yet to meet the perfect person, or the perfect home. The purpose of the home inspection process is to conduct a search for what is right and what is wrong. Unfortunately, in many cases home inspectors only emphasize what is wrong with a home. Be sure to maintain a good perspective on what you will be gaining, knowing that all houses will have some "issues."

The Importance of Legal Representation

Over the years questions have been raised over the need for legal representation in a real estate transaction. In my view, all real estate transactions should have the benefit of a professional legal review. In some parts of the country, escrow companies will close the transaction and provide legal assistance in the process. In the event a problem should arise, it would be foolish to try to solve it without having qualified legal help. Many attorneys specialize in real estate, and their support staff is dedicated to helping make the transition a smooth one. Relative to other kinds of legal charges, the fees associated with the buying and selling process are quite reasonable for normal closings. Always ask up front what those charges are going to be and consider them part of your total estimated closing costs. When you consider the financial and legal responsibilities associated with home ownership, it makes good sense to have your own attorney. Third-party professionals on the team are there to be sure everything goes right, but their true value may come into play if things turn in the wrong direction. That's another kind of insurance you'll want to have.

A Funnel Tells the Story

Think of the shape of a funnel. It can serve as an analogy to explain buyer "flow." If we place the funnel down with the wide part on table we have a shape that appears like a cone with a long tube at the end. At the beginning levels of the market you have the highest number of buyers in the marketplace, represented by the widest part of the funnel shape. As you work your way up that funnel it starts to get smaller and smaller. In the middle of the funnel you have fewer buyers than you do at the widest part. As home prices increase the actual number of buyers and homes available starts to decrease. Therefore as you approach the entrance to the narrowest part of the funnel, you are now viewing the most limited number of buyers available for the most expensive homes in the world. Fewer homes, fewer buyers. However, although the number of buyers is the smallest here, the actual purchasing power may be the highest. As you approach the very end of the funnel you are dealing with the most expensive homes in the country and the smallest percentage of the buyers who can afford to purchase them.

HOW THE INTERNET
HAS CHANGED EVERYTHING

Regardless of who claims he has invented the internet, it is here and it is going to stay. We have a whole generation of people who use the internet for just about everything. The amount of information available is mind-boggling. It's like being able to tap into the biggest brain on the planet.

Real estate companies have been quick to get on the internet express. Websites now provide all the access you need to seek mortgage information, brokers, assistance programs, and, of course, homes. There are thousands of homes, all available online from anywhere in the country. You can sit in your chair and view homes for days. You can take a "virtual tour" while sitting in your den. You do not even have to go to see these homes. You can form your opinions just by looking at the pictures or videos. What a time saver for buyers and sellers. Or is it?

The Internet Highway Has Some Potholes, Too

Finding a home is similar to looking for a perfect mate. Simply join one of those popular "personal" sites online and you can search for the perfect life partner. You can list the physical attributes, special common interests, philosophies, life goals, and other information necessary to find your match. Hit the "send" button and you're on your way—or so you think. Thousands of people across the country spend hours on internet personal sites looking over the candidates only to be disappointed when they meet their "match" in person. Why does this happen? "Chemistry" is the answer. It does not transmit over the internet. It cannot be conveyed in a photograph. It has to happen when two people meet in person. You will know it when you have it and you will know it when you don't.

Believe it or not, almost the same thing happens to people searching for the house of their dreams via the internet. Buyers can type in what they can afford to pay each month, as well as the number of bedrooms, baths, and other features that they are seeking. Push "send" and presto! The home of your dreams appears right in front of you. Schedule the closing and your search is over. Unfortunately, it rarely happens this way. Chemistry is an important part of the home search, too.

This is not to say that the internet is not useful to the potential home buyer. Legal and financial information is widely available, and many buyers determine their estimated mortgage qualifications through lender websites. (Which is why I haven't spent a lot of time providing information in this book that can be easily obtained online.)

It's fine to do your research on real estate websites, but always remember that purchasing a home requires a certain amount of "fieldwork" as well. If you spend a full day with a true expert viewing and walking actual properties, it will be clear that both online and on-the-ground research are necessary. A great photograph rarely tells the entire story. Keep in mind that most property photographs are taken to create interest, not turn it off.

The same thing applies to real estate agents as well. An agent who only works the internet is not serving his client well. What appears to be a time saver can turn out to be a time waster. Agents have to find homes that turn them on in order to deliver the service and timing every customer deserves. Agents need to preview properties in person, not in front of a screen. Not knowing a product up close is a sure way to decrease the chances of success. The "shotgun" approach— "If I show enough properties to enough people, eventually they will find one they like"—only shows that an agent hasn't made the effort to preview properties and narrow down the list of possibilities for a potential buyer. Talk about firing at a blank target.

The Sun Came Up on My Son

Recently my son just bought his first home. He has a very demanding job and literally no time during his work day to look for a home. So the internet sure looked like the best way to view some properties. What a time-saver it appeared to be for him. After work he spent hours looking at homes online. He even thought he had a good feel for prices. Then he sent some of them over to me to review. I told him this was not the way to go about looking for a home. He was not ready to listen quite yet, and the internet appeared to be helping, at least on the surface. He drove by several homes, but none of them appeared the way he had imagined them from their online profiles. What appeared to be a time saver actually turned out to be just a partial picture of the market. Frustrated and seeking help, he was now ready to begin the process of becoming a real buyer.

Patience can be a virtue, especially with your own kids. My patience paid off because I learned a long time ago that it is a lot easier to go through an open door than a closed one. I met with John and explained how to go about looking for a home. He took my advice and followed all the steps outlined in this book. He began his search for a top-level broker in the area with my assistance. We found the perfect agent to help him. His name was Tom, and he fit the profile perfectly. This set up the business meeting, which allowed John to focus on his purchase. He learned everything he needed to know and all the potential properties were directed to fit his particular situation. That kind of concentration can create all the right stuff for becoming a true buyer. You have to stop and sit down with an expert if you want to soften the learning curve. How do I fit the market and how does the market fit me? These are two important questions that have to be answered, and they were. Tom had done his job.

Let's cut to the chase on this story. Pre-approved and ready to put that check book to work, he looked at homes in a well thought-out plan. He looked at some homes under what he could spend, and others just over what he could afford. He gained the knowledge and confidence to purchase his first home prudently.

After weeks of looking around on the internet, he spent one day with this agent and found the home of his dreams. The house had three other offers on it, but John wanted the place, not "second place." He got the home. Just luck? No way.

Preparation, knowledge, and execution all combined to make it happen. Not a bad day at all.

The internet is a fabulous tool. It may well turn out to be one of the best tools in the shed. But tools alone cannot replace the personal touch necessary for successful home transactions. It's a people business. People build homes, people live in homes, and people sell homes. When it comes to the internet, there is nothing like it for gaining information and in some areas, saving an enormous amount of time. Use it to your advantage but do not use it as the only means to buy or sell a home.

BUYING FOR
INVESTMENT ONLY

I was only married for about ten months when the idea of paying rent started to nag at me. We were living in a nice two-family duplex, basically half a house. I desired privacy badly. I guess it would have been OK if I'd owned it. Home ownership, just the sound of it, gives you a feeling of pride.

It was not very long before we found that dilapidated, vacant 1806 farmhouse. You know the rest of that story. We left the duplex and headed for our first home. What I did not add earlier was that about five years after buying the farmhouse and building the equity, I had the opportunity to buy that two-family duplex we lived in when we were first married. I knew the property, I knew the owner and I knew it would be a good deal. So we bought it. It was a good place, but it needed some work. I spruced up both units, gave the outside plenty of curb appeal and raised the rent on both sides to a combined increase of $350.00 per month. In doing that, I immediately increased the value of the investment property. In less than six months I had increased the value of the property by over $15,000. I now had an extra monthly income and some more equity. It was that extra income that gave me the confidence to sell the farm house and move to that new home on the cul-de-sac. Keep in mind all these figures are from around 1972. The numbers would be higher now, but the concept would still be valid. If you understand the principles of real estate you can apply them anytime, anywhere.

As it turned out, I kept that duplex for many years. I was able to raise the rent with every new tenant. That single investment changed the landscape for me forever. I went on to buy many other investment properties. All of them had "good bones" but needed some hard work to bring them back to life. I bought them, fixed them up, and rented them for income and equity growth. It worked for me just like it had worked for my parents. At one point I owned ten residential properties and personally managed them all. I did the maintenance myself, except for the occasional item I couldn't handle. I also maintained a high-level management position in the second largest independently-owned residential real estate company in America. I never once went to court, or had a serious problem with any tenant.

Let me elaborate on that last sentence.

The Best "Home Rule" Is the Golden Rule

People have asked me how I avoided the normal problems of landlord-tenant relations. After all, with a group of properties and some of them duplexes, I sure had a pretty good basket of tenants. The answer was simple for me.

First of all, I never considered myself to be a landlord. That term did not register in my mind. Somehow it appeared less than what I was. I was the owner of the property. I had pride in what I owned and wanted to keep any house I owned in good shape, not just for the tenant, but for me. Therein lay a significant difference in my attitude from other property owners. Where most owners of investment real estate go wrong is that they are only interested in the rent coming in on time. That's a very narrow view of the benefits of investment property ownership.

Appreciation of a property's value will happen if the land values keep going up. However, if you let a home "go" for years and years without proper maintenance, the value of the property can diminish significantly. So while you may get rent on time, you may be losing one or two percent a year on the appreciation. On a house worth $375,000 that's close to $5,000 each year. Deduct that from the rent roll and the picture becomes a bit clearer for the residential investor. Why gain on one side only to lose on the other?

Secondly, I approached all my prospective occupants not as tenants but as people who were going to live in my house. I wanted them to be comfortable. I wanted them to be happy. I wanted them to like me and therefore like the house. It all works together. I have known situations where the tenant was so angry at the landlord that they actually caused damage to the property to get even. It happens every day. Whenever I would rent a property I would always make an allowance for something the prospective tenant wanted to do to the house. I would buy paint, wallpaper, or any other needed amenities. After all, if I got the labor for free, why would I not want to improve my own place? It was not logical for me to do anything differently. This first "act of kindness" on my part helped to form a team between me and the people living in my house. When they would call with a problem, I would thank them for calling me. I would take care of it at the same fast pace I would if the problem occurred in the house I was living in. Why not? I owned them both.

Many times after a family would leave one of my properties, they would point out all the little things they had done to improve the house or repair an item that had been broken. They said and I quote, "You were so nice to us, we did not want to bother you with small issues, so we took care of them ourselves." It was a good relationship because I started it off on the right note, a note of harmony. The golden rule works fabulously with ownership of residential investment properties.

To this day I do not think of myself as landlord. Maintaining any property on a regular basis will bring greater rewards than letting its condition deteriorate. Just because you don't live in it is no excuse to let it run down. You can take care of problems as they come up, or wait until repairs cost significantly more. There used to be a transmission repair television commercial that aptly stated, "You can pay me now or you can pay me later." The same can be said of investment property maintenance.

Maintaining a rental property also directly affects the amount of rent you can expect to receive. When you're renting a property that's in top condition, your chances of receiving the highest rent possible improve. Your property stands out from other properties. Shelf position counts with rentals, too. An attractive property attracts a higher paying tenant, which in turn gives you the extra money needed to keep the property in excellent condition. It can be a very nice circle of success for everyone.

You Will Get Paid Well for Your Time

Real estate investments are not for everyone. Over the

years many people have steered away from them because of horror stories associated with the landlord/tenant relationship. In my experience, it doesn't have to be that way.

On occasion you will have to work. Just like your career, managing your investment properties requires work and responsibility. As the owner of residential investment properties, your responsibilities might include: meeting potential renters, showing the property, drawing simple leases, making deposits of security funds, working with a realtor, changing keys, locks, painting, normal home maintenance repairs, and a minimal amount of paperwork each month. If significant improvements are needed, they will usually pay off handsomely in higher rent, a more attractive property, and increased market value.

One of the main problems associated with owning rental properties is that most owners never want to hear from their tenants. They just want the rent paid on time. On occasion when a renter calls with a problem, the owner takes it as a major inconvenience. "Who needs this? Just when I was sitting down to eat I get a call telling me there's a problem with the toilet." Yes, you will have some problems, just like you do everyday at your regular job. At work you expect it because each month you bring home a paycheck. Guess what? The investment property sends home a paycheck, too. That rental check is not hay. Imagine calling your boss and telling him you don't want to hear about any problems at work, at the same time insisting that you want to get paid on time!

When you consider all the income earned and then add in the tax benefits, depreciation deduction, and property appreciation, you just might find that your investment property is paying you more per hour than your career job. I had many a year when an investment property earned me over $750 per hour, and that was some time ago. All in all, the number of hours worked was few. Some of those calls may have come at inconvenient times, but when the rent check arrived, it was never inconvenient.

19 HOME SWEET
"SAVINGS & LOAN HOME"

In a previous section in this book I covered how a home can actually turn out to be your own private "savings and loan." It does not take many years for equity to build. Leveraging the increasing market value of your home allows you to borrow more against it, a situation in which you are effectively lending yourself money.

"Home Sweet Home" never sounds better than when you need money for an addition, debt consolidation, or a college education. It's worth seeing how quickly your equity can actually build up. Let's say you purchased a house in 2004 for $300,000. You put down 20%, or $60,000, meaning that you took out a mortgage of $240,000. For the ease of figures we will say the mortgage was at 6%, and was a fixed 30-year loan.

For the first five years of ownership we will assume that the home will appreciate at 5% a year. At the end of one year the home therefore would be worth about $315,000. At the end of the second year it would be valued at $330,750, the third year $347, 300, the fourth year $364,655, and at the end of five years the home would have a market value of $382,900.

The result is a total gain in value of $82,900, or an average of just about $16,600 a year. This is based on no additional improvements to the home, simply maintaining the residence in good condition. Saving $16,600 each year while you are living in your home is a fantastic accomplishment for most people.

Now let's factor in the reduction of the mortgage principal after just five years. In the early years of a mortgage, most of the monthly payment will go to pay for the interest on the loan, but each month there is a reduction of the principal amount borrowed as well. The typical monthly mortgage statement will show the interest paid and the balance of the loan principal as of the last payment. The total monthly payment on a mortgage of $240,000 at 6% interest with a 30 year payout would be about $1,440 per month. The principal balance at the end of 5 years would be $223,440—a pay down of $16,560 in just five years. That works out to an approximate principal payoff each year of $3,312.

Equity Gains Build Your Assets

To sum up, the total equity gain at the end of just 5 years of ownership would be as follows:

1.   *Principal reduced by $16,560 from original loan amount, leaving a loan balance of: $223,440.*

2.   *Home appreciation figured at 5% per year amounts to $82,900 in increased market value of the home.*

3.   *Equity available: Value of $382,900 minus loan balance of $223,440 leaves a total equity amount of: $159,460.*

Summary: In 5 years your original down payment of $60,000 has increased by almost $100,000. That converts to an average annual savings of approximately $20,000 each year.

You now have a substantial amount of equity available for loan purposes. Home equity loans are always very competitive and the homeowner usually has many types of loans to choose from. Using the standard guideline that 80% of a home's value may be available to borrow against; this home could support $300,000 in loans to a qualified owner. If interest rates have fallen since the initial purchase, the entire mortgage could be refinanced.

Staying with this example, let's revisit the tax advantages of home ownership. In addition to the savings gained from market appreciation and loan principal payoff, real estate taxes are tax deductible. For the purposes of this exercise we will state the real estate taxes to be $6,000 per year. If you are in the 30% tax bracket, you would realize $1,800 (30% of $6,000) as a deduction. Because taxes usually go up each year, for the five-year period we will estimate the average taxes at approximately $6,500 per year. This yields an average tax deduction of $1,950 each year, or a total of $9,750 for the five-year period. There is more. The interest paid on this mortgage is also tax deductible and offers another great tax advantage for homeowners. Assume that out of the $1,440 monthly mortgage payment approximately $275 was the average principal payment for the five years. That leaves an average interest payment of about $14,000 each year. If you are in the 30% tax bracket you would be able to deduct a further $4,200 from your taxes.

The Final Recap

Over the five-year period the following can happen:

1. *Mortgage principal reduced by:$16,560*

2. *Home market appreciation of:$82,900*

3. *Equity in the home: $159,469*

4. *Cash growth: The initial down payment of $60,000 has become worth $159,469. That is a $100,000 gain.*

4. *Tax savings from mortgage interest paid: $21,000 ($4,200 each of the five years)*

5. *Tax savings from real estate taxes paid: $9,750 ($1,950 each of the five years)*

Add it all up and you can see why "Making the Right Moves in Real Estate" can really build assets. Between appreciation, principal pay-off, and tax savings, the total impact of our "model" home would be an impressive $130,210!

FROM THE KITCHEN DRAWER: REAL ESTATE ETHICS THEN AND NOW

The Good Old Days Were Not All So Good

During the 1950s and 1960s there were few multi-office residential real estate companies. Most were small offices with a few agents. Usually there was a main broker, a few full-time agents, and who knows how many part-timers on an office roster. Most agencies were named after the principal broker. Furthermore, there was literally no on-the-job training of agents. If you were fortunate enough to have a broker that wanted to break you in, your training might have lasted a few hours. You learned as you went along.

The real estate business in those days was characterized by the tried but true expression, "buyer beware." The seller of a property could do just about anything he or she wanted to get the house sold and not have to worry about any legal repercussions. What you saw is what you got and if you did not see it, you got it anyway! At that time it was not uncommon for each broker to have what were known as "pocket listings," or properties that only one broker knew about and did not share with other brokers. It was a simple "it is my listing and I will sell it" mentality. (I remember being shown the same property by two different brokers at two different prices in New York state many years ago. I guess that would have been a "two-pocket" listing.)

Fortunately, these dubious practices did not survive. With the growth of multiple listing services and the development of rules and regulations protecting the consumer, industry practices began to improve. The multiple listing services were determined to make the playing field level for all buyers, sellers, and agents.

Nothing has helped the consumer more than the multiple listing services. The National Association of Realtors has established strong guidelines for its members. In addition, broker awareness that training programs are the key to improving an agent's professionalism have added to the high level of services available to the consumer. Competition in the real estate field was one of the key reasons that brokers developed the tools and training necessary to attract and keep the best agents. The largest companies were the first to institute these measures and set an example for smaller firms nationwide.

A True Story

Many years ago there was a wonderful salesman who worked with me in a local real estate office. Everyone just loved him because he had an incredible sense of humor. One day, a bunch of us piled into a car to preview a home in the area. As we pulled up to the listing the immediate reaction was that the house was overpriced. As we walked the property it became even more evident to all of us. It wasn't just overpriced, it was way overpriced. Then the salesman saw three kids watching television in the living room. He walked up to them and asked, "Are you having a good time?" They looked up and in unison said, "Yes." He then went on to ask them if they liked living there. Again, the kids replied in unison, "Yes we do." The salesman then said, "Good, because you're going to be here for a long, long time." Holding our laughs until we all got back in the car was not easy.

Still Another True Tale

While waiting for another broker to meet me at a home, my clients wanted to see the backyard. As it turned out, the owner was home, but he was busy outside painting some second floor windows. I greeted him and introduced myself and the clients. He said he would be right down to let us in the home. I noticed that he had left a can of paint next to the ladder, but I didn't think much about it. As he got to the bottom of the ladder, he turned to say something, but accidentally tripped and in doing so kicked the half-full can of paint over on its side. He fell on to the brick patio, but fortunately was not hurt. To lighten the moment I remarked that "kicking the bucket" may not be such a bad thing after all.

The Best Agents Know It Is a People Business

Over the years I have heard numerous real estate agents say, "I am so glad I recently moved, because it has helped me to stay in touch with what my buyers and sellers experience."

There is a lot of truth in that statement. Perhaps realtors should be required to move every five years or so. Obviously, sales associates should not have to physically relocate to keep in tune with their clients, but agents that have moved recently all agree that it really does help them maintain a keen sensitivity to the needs of their buyers and sellers.

People move, not houses. People make the process work, and therefore superior communication skills are needed at every level. The best way to work with people is to treat them all fairly and listen carefully to their needs and desires. Treat them like you want to be treated. It's that simple. Real estate agents who focus their efforts on helping their buyers and sellers accomplish their goals are building a lifetime referral base.

A Trip to the Local Grocery Store Can Provide a Good Test of Service

After many years of selling real estate, I've concluded that there is one sure way for sales agents to test their own customer service performance. For the most part, real estate is a very local business. The product is local, and the people selling homes are local, living and working in the same neighborhoods as their clients. Unlike other industries, which may have a state, regional, or international base, real estate customers are right in your own backyard. Therefore real estate sales people have an additional responsibility to their community and neighbors. It pays many times over to leave a crystal clear trail of service. If you are an agent, a very simple but worthwhile self-test of your own sales performance can be made by simply asking one key question. "When I go to the local grocery store, are there any past or present customers I would have to avoid?" If the answer is no, then you have passed the test because you have treated your clients fairly and professionally.

21 THE HOUSE TOUR
COMES TO AN END

Though market conditions and interest rates will always fluctuate, home ownership will be the foundation of people's lives for years to come. I can't think of one reason why the desire to own a home will not continue to be a driving force for most people. Real estate not only provides shelter, but also helps us to establish our lifestyle.

When my daughter Allison was about two years old, she slept in a room in our old farmhouse that had fairly low ceilings; in fact, she could stand up in her crib and touch the beams, which made her feel safe and secure. After reading to her at night, she would always ask me to "yeave the yights on." Being a concerned Daddy I would always leave the lights on. As she snuggled into her bed and felt the comfort of her room all around her, Allison knew there was no place like home, and I knew it, too!

History has shown us that home ownership can provide us with a variety of opportunities. We can entertain our friends and family and build a life style around our values and beliefs. Home ownership also provides a wonderful chance to become active contributors within a community. For many, it provides the perfect setting to meet and develop new and meaningful relationships. Decorating your own special place can also provide the canvas on which you express your own creativity and/or point of view. For most of us, a home is a security blanket that can provide a sanctuary from the hectic pace of our culture. There are other proven investments that can help build your family assets, but I don't know of any other that can combine all of the benefits of real estate.

The Back Door

Armed with the knowledge and commitment of how to better navigate your way through the world of real estate, this book can serve as a permanent guide for millions of buyers, sellers and real estate professionals. Building your assets with real estate is an honorable goal. It can be reached by anyone determined enough to plan ahead, gain the benefits of disciplined savings and willing to make a few sacrifices, for their own betterment. "Making the Right Moves in Real Estate" is one of the best ways to insure success.

As we close the "back door" on this book, your cart should be full with the building blocks necessary to establish the foundation upon which successful real estate transactions are built. What also matters is that you will have the courage, determination, and sense of urgency necessary to make your own real estate moves count the most. Remember that knowledge learned and never applied in the real world, is like practicing for a game that will never be played.

22 SHORT LESSONS
FROM LONG JOURNEYS

Quick reminders that help me keep the balance in my life:

Experts in the same field rarely agree on anything.

❋

Opinions are just that, opinions.

❋

Chain reactions work best when they are planned.

❋

Money is important, but not at any cost.

❋

Teamwork is not something you can do alone.

❋

Lending your neighbor your spirit can lift yours.

❋

A good attitude always improves the view.

❋

Talking gets in the way of listening and learning.

The best house in the neighborhood may
not have the happiest people inside.

❋

Running away from a problem only increases the
speed at which the problem will follow you.

❋

Compromise is the stuff that binds relationships.

❋

Worry drains good energy and creates imaginary
problems, most of which will never occur.

❋

Life is like a lot of great books; not
all chapters are happy ones.

❋

Do not put off doing something today that you should have
done yesterday because you think it will go away tomorrow.

❋

Having faith in your own future is the key to having a future.

❋

Building wealth is a combination of
accumulating and preserving.

❋

Before you spend all of your time "lining up
your ducks," be sure you own the pond.

Either you manage your money or it will manage you.

❋

Timing comes in many varieties, but

bad timing is the worst kind.

❋

Taking the quick and easy way out usually

leads to the long and hard way back.

❋

Many bad decisions are driven by greed, not ignorance.

❋

The more people you ask about a decision,

the less chance you have of making one.

❋

In the end, we all work for ourselves.

❋

When you challenge the benefits of teamwork, think of

how each grain of sand works together, to create a beach.

❋

"The best 'dividends' come from investing in others"

About the Author

Richard Ardia started his career as a high school teacher. After seven years he had coached, taught, and participated on many different educational levels but something was still missing. He went into the real estate business in 1972 and within a short period of time, became the number one sales associate in a company of over 100 agents. He immediately started purchasing investment real estate and out of necessity became a skilled tradesman in home repairs.

He joined a local six-office real estate company in 1978 and as the executive vice president of that firm, quickly combined his business and teaching skills. Ardia was instrumental in bringing agent and management training to the industry. He participated in the early stages of educational development in a field hungry for knowledge. He created and delivered numerous marketing tools and was well known for his instructional and inspirational speeches.

Over the next 13 years he participated in the decisions that made that company grow to over 100 offices in five states. Richard Ardia was best known for his "steel like" ethics and integrity. He never changed his personal dedication to helping others discover their talents and grow accordingly.

Showing career versatility, Ardia became the president of a niche manufacturing company with about 85 employees. With a strong management team in place, the company broke their 40-year sales record. He learned that regardless of the product, it is always the efforts of the people that matter the most.

The author owned several of his own companies. He was the originator of the Broker Search Connection, a company that specialized in finding the best agents available with out any restrictions as to broker affiliations. Ardia also was the owner of a property management company which managed residential homes, condominium associations, and provided maintenance services to their clients.

"Most of my life I have dreamed of writing a book that would project the most honest and forthright benefits of home ownership. I learned first hand that *Making the Right Moves in Real Estate* made a significant difference in my life. Sharing information with others, so that they can better navigate their lives, is one of life's true pleasures. We are here to participate. There may not always be a pot of gold at the end of every rainbow but you sure can't beat the view."